Madison Avenue Maxi

Madison Avenue

axi

ELKE GAZZARA

CARROLL & GRAF PUBLISHERS
NEW YORK

Madison Avenue Maxi

Carroll & Graf Publishers
11 Cambridge Center, Cambridge, MA 02142

AVALON
publishing group, incorporated

Library of Congress Cataloging-in-Publication Data is available.

ISBN-13: 978-0-7867-2038-5
ISBN-10: 0-7867-2038-7

9 8 7 6 5 4 3 2 1

Book design by Pauline Neuwirth, Neuwirth & Associates, Inc.

Printed in the United States of America

For Ben—
and, of course,
Maxi

Acknowledgments

THANKS TO my editor, Don Weise; my agent, Jennifer Lyons; my friend, Lynn Ryker; and special thanks to Douglas Ladnier for his support throughout my work on this book. And my deep appreciation to my daughter, Danja, for bringing us our precious Maxi.

Contents

Madison Avenue Maxi

Madison Avenue

ᴹADISON AVENUE IS where I live with my husband, actor Ben Gazzara. It is also where I browse and shop. Our dog Maxi, a short-haired, sable-colored miniature dachshund, is usually with me and always dressed her best as I walk the avenue. There's not a morning when I don't have trouble choosing her collar and leash. She has dozens of each. Like a mother who spoils her child, I've given Maxi too much of everything, so she looks forward to her visits to the chic boutiques along the avenue. We often stop at Missoni, where a big couch is always waiting for her to lie on while I look around. And further down the avenue are the dog-friendly stores Donna Karan, Dolce & Gabbana, Chanel, Gucci, Valentino, and Hermès. A husband's nightmare.

But one morning, our visits to the store had to wait. I wound up in the emergency room of the Lenox Hill Hospital with severe abdominal pains. There were too many examinations, including two MRIs. And then the waiting began.

In twenty-five years, I have never been to a doctor without Ben. Suddenly, here I was alone with my darling little dog and with my doctor, who did not have good news.

"Where is Ben?" he asked.

I told him that my husband had just begun rehearsing a revival of Clifford Odets' *Awake and Sing*, which would soon open on Broadway.

"I wish Ben were here," he continued. "We may need to talk to him too."

"What is it, doctor?"

"Well, you don't have kidney stones, my dear."

"Good. And?"

"You have a growth on your pancreas. It looks like a tumor."

My heart was in my throat. "Doctor, do you mean it's cancer?"

He looked at me for some time and said, "I hope not, but it doesn't look good."

"Can it be operated on?"

"Today many things can be done," he said not too convincingly.

I had the feeling suddenly as if someone had slammed a fist in my stomach. I took Maxi out of her bag and noticed her quick heartbeat as she looked up at me. I was scared and my tears began to flow. Maxi quietly and tenderly licked them away. Still I couldn't move. The thought of having cancer was making me dizzy.

"There are more tests we can do," said Dr. Orsher. "You'll see Dr. Knapp in a few minutes. He's expecting you."

And with that he kissed me on the forehead and said, "We'll get through this, my dear. We'll find a way."

My life had been turned upside down. These should have been my happiest moments. We were back in New York after many months in Italy and Ben was working with some very fine actors and a brilliant director on a play he loved. I left the doctor's office with Maxi still in my arms and stepped into the familiar sunshine of Seventy-ninth Street. I could not stop trembling as I walked the five doors down to Dr. Knapp, another one of our favorite and too-frequent doctors.

Dr. Knapp was waiting for me.

"Elke, come in. Ben is not with you?"

"Ben is working. What is the news, Dr. Knapp?"

"The news is not so good."

"How bad is not so good?"

"My darling Elke, you don't have a kidney stone," he said, trying to lighten my spirits.

"I know doctor. I have a growth on my pancreas. Is it cancer?"

"Let's do some more tests immediately. I have the lab reserved for you. It's right around the corner on Seventy-eighth Street. My nurse will give you the address."

"Dr. Knapp, when will we have the results?"

"They'll phone me later today and I'll call you immediately."

"Thank you doctor."

He embraced me and said good luck.

At that moment, Ben called me from his rehearsal asking how things had gone at the doctor. I did not want to upset him and tell him my troubles while he was working, so I said everything was fine. I knew that if I told him the truth, he would leave rehearsal—even quit the play—to be with me night and day. What a mess.

Before heading to another exhaustive examination, I walked Maxi along Madison Avenue toward our home. We passed our local grade school, PS 6, and found ourselves surrounded by a group of school-children. A few of them came up to us.

"May I pet her?" asked one adorable-looking boy.

"Yes, you may," I said, "but go slowly."

"What's his name?" asked one little girl, referring to Maxi.

"It's a she," I said.

"What's *her* name?" asked the girl.

"Maxi. Her name is Maxi," I said, biting my tongue to hold back my tears.

When we arrived at home, my maid Geeta came running to the door and asked, "Mrs. G., how's it going? What did the doctor say?" She knew how much pain I'd been in. I didn't have to say a word. I handed Maxi to Geeta, telling her to please give her a piece of raw carrot once in a while and fresh water. I wish they'd give me fresh water instead of the pink cement I'd have to drink before my CAT scan. Not only did I have to drink it, but I spent nearly two hours inside a tube with IVs in my arms pumping the pink fluid into my veins. It had always been one of my favorite colors, but this time, I didn't feel so pretty in pink. I thought only of Ben and Maxi. Seeing their faces helped me handle this claustrophobic and very difficult moment. Each time the doctor told me to hold my breath so he could take his picture, often for too long a time, I would breathe in Maxi and breathe out Ben.

I left the doctor's office with my friend Lisa Tobin, who had rushed over to be with me. What a couple we were. She was on crutches with a freshly operated-on kneecap and I was walking next to her feeling like a bloated zombie, waiting for the prognosis from my doctors. I knew that if I had cancer of the pancreas, I would not live. Soon I may never see and embrace Ben again or play with my little Maxi.

We waited anxiously at a nearby restaurant for the call. It seemed like an eternity. As the soup was served, my cell phone rang. I moved to an empty corner of the restaurant. It was Geeta.

"Mrs. G., Mrs. G. your doctor phoned. Here is his cell phone number."

I immediately phoned Dr. Knapp.

"Congratulations Elke. You are better than we thought. You don't have cancer. Your pancreas is badly inflamed because you have a handful of gallstones. This will be a simple operation."

"Doctor, this is the best news! I could dance on the table. What do I do now?"

"No alcohol and don't eat anything fatty. I'll phone in some prescriptions. Come to my office on Monday. You're going to be fine."

Almost flying, I returned to Lisa with both thumbs up and a big smile. All I had were some little rocks in my gallbladder. If they had been boulders, I would have still celebrated.

MAXI MUST HAVE missed me while I was gone. She hadn't eaten a single cookie Geeta offered her. She licked my face excitedly when I came through the door with her familiar, high-pitched bark. "I love you, I love you, I love you." It was as though she sensed everything was going to be all right.

Meet Max

$\mathcal{T}$HE FIRST TIME I saw Maxi, I actually couldn't see her at all. My husband and I were sitting at an outside table waiting for my daughter to join us for lunch at La Goulue on Madison Avenue. When Danja arrived, she immediately sat down and opened the zipper of her large, green shoulder bag.

"Meet Max," she said.

"Who's Max?" Ben asked.

Just then a little brown something popped its head out of Danja's bag.

"Max is my dog."

Looking down at the tiny creature, Ben laughed. "That's not a dog, it's a mouse."

Over lunch, we learned that Danja was in love; but not just with Max. She was playing house with a new boyfriend in her apartment on Central Park South, and the dog was their new baby. Max had

arrived only days before from a breeder in Missouri and, at ten weeks old, did indeed look more like a chocolate mouse than a dog.

At some point during lunch, Danja excused herself to the restroom and pushed the bag near my feet under the table to hide the dog from the waiters. "Take care of Max, I'll be right back," she said to me in German, our secret language.

Thank God we were at an outside table or this dog could get us in trouble, I thought.

After Danja was safely gone, Ben looked at me and said, "It'll never last. I bet you that when that love affair is over, that dog is gonna be our dog."

"If only," I said, secretly hoping; I'd been pushing Ben to get a dog for years.

"You will see. But remember, I don't want a dog."

Too late. It had already started. I had fallen in love with Max.

Suddenly I was a young grandmother, more interested in rubber chewies and liver treats than baby booties and high-chairs, but a grandmother nonetheless. And I took my new role very seriously. My handbag was always stuffed with squeaking balls or gourmet dog cookies in every shape and color just in case I saw Max. I ordered books on miniature dachshunds, coffee mugs with dachshunds, dachshund calendars, and even a pair of dachshund floor mats, one for Danja and one for me. I bought everything that had a dachshund on it: napkins, handbags, key chains, Hermès ashtrays, even dachshund brooches. Finally, when I arrived with a dachshund iron door-stop, Danja said, "Mommy stop. It's enough. We have a living Max."

Having a dog around sometimes brought a new playfulness to my life. I couldn't wait for Danja to call me for an afternoon stroll in Central Park or an impromptu "girls' lunch" because I knew Max would be there, too. Danja educated Maxi well from the beginning. Not only was Max potty and paper trained, but she also learned from an early age to sit silently in her bag while we dined in many of New York's not-so-dog-friendly restaurants. She behaved so well when we were out in public that it seemed very easy to have a dog.

Danja was a working girl, and her boyfriend worked, too. Max was sometimes left alone in the kitchen for up to nine hours during the day. As good of a girl as Max is, she doesn't like to be left alone—even to this day. Though she often entertained herself by playing with a ball, she would also chew and claw the kitchen door if left alone too long. In fact, she once scratched so long and hard on an iron blockade keeping her locked in the kitchen that she was bleeding from her paws and her nose when Danja arrived home. Danja relayed these and many happier stories to me on the telephone while Ben and I were on location in Europe for some months. During this time, my conversations with Danja were more than ninety percent about Max. She was the proud mom filling in the proud grandma.

I remember Danja calling once to share with me Max's first words. Danja spoke first in a high-pitched voice that sounded more like a squeal, saying, "I love you, I love you, I love you."

When Max promptly interrupted with her own even squeakier, "I love you, I love you, I love you too."

Within just a few months, in late November, Danja's new family was already beginning to fall apart. She and Max needed an escape from the city for a few days and asked if they could join Ben and me for a long weekend at our home in Sag Harbor. I was excited!

It was a beautiful winter weekend with warm sunshine and high snow. Max was eight months old by now, and she played like a schoolgirl in her first snow, jumping around like a little kangaroo or a bunny rabbit. I was in love. "Ben, look at Max. What an adorable little dog. Oh *Gott, sie ist so süss.*"

Ben was bundled up on the porch sitting with his coffee and the *New York Times*, enjoying the morning sun. Without looking up and not missing a beat, he said, "Don't start. I don't want a dog."

Danja called me into the house. I could tell that something was wrong. I had seen something sad in her face all weekend and now perhaps she was finally ready to open up to me. "Mommy, I have to talk to you. My boyfriend and I are splitting up. In fact, he won't be there when I get home tomorrow."

"Are you all right?"

"Yes," she said quietly.

"Is there anything I can do *mein kind?*"

"Well, actually yes. I'd like to go back to the city by myself tomorrow and leave Max with you for a couple of days if you don't mind."

"I don't know if that's a good idea, Danja. Ben would not like it."

"It's only a couple of days, Mommy. It's your home too and she's just a little dog—she's no trouble at all. Please?"

"Okay, okay. Let me talk to Ben. Only two days, Danja. We will see."

After a few "I told you so's" and some minor grunts and grumbles from my husband, Ben and I had our first weekend alone with Max.

Our first outing was dinner in the American Hotel. We sat by the fireplace long into the evening laughing, talking, and drinking with friends. Max was so good and quiet in her travel bag that nobody even noticed we had a dog with us. I was hoping that Ben might even forget. At some point when the night was winding down, I opened the bag to share Max with our friends—they couldn't believe she had been sitting so silently all night.

"What a beautiful dog! Congratulations! When did you get her?"

"Congratulations to our daughter. It's her dog," Ben quickly replied.

I was disappointed but not hopeless. Without him knowing, I had seen Ben sneak little bites to Max three times during dinner. I could tell he was softening. That night on our way home, I watched with pleasure as Ben gently covered a sleeping Max with his sweater to keep her warm.

The next day, Max came with us for lunch and even sat quietly through an entire afternoon movie at our local theater before retiring with us for a peaceful evening at home. While I was preparing Ben's favorite pasta *alla puttanesca*, I sent him upstairs to watch his sports; Max stayed downstairs with me hoping to catch any morsels or crumbs I might drop. I got the idea to take her upstairs and put her on Ben's lap, hoping he would get used to her and maybe even begin to like having her around.

"Ben, could you hold her while I finish cooking? She wants to eat everything she sees me chop. Wouldn't she be better up here with you?"

"Stick her in her bag. She likes it there."

"She was in her bag the whole afternoon, Ben. Please. Let her sit with you. She might like sports, too."

"Okay. Put her here," he said, gesturing to his lap.

Max settled in nicely. It warmed my heart.

During dinner, I asked Ben, "Wouldn't you like to have a sweet little animal like that of our own someday?"

"I will only say it once. The answer is no."

The lovely evening had taken a sad turn.

The next day, our friend Richard drove us back to New York from Sag Harbor. Max slept on Ben's lap the entire ride home. I sat in the back seat of the car wishing we would drive straight to our apartment on Madison Avenue without returning Max to Danja. Watching the New York skyline get bigger and bigger as we came closer to the city, I felt so happy and hopeful about my new little family. Everything was almost perfect. If only we had a little dog of our own.

Cutting my fantasy short, Ben growled, "Central Park South."

I thought my heart would stop. Ben wanted to take Max straight home to Danja.

And that was it. Our first solo adventure with Max was finished.

I DIDN'T HEAR from Danja for two days. When she phoned, she told me that Max hadn't been eating, drinking, or sleeping well since we dropped her off. She began to suggest that Max would be happier in our care than in hers. I knew Danja wanted to go out and paint the town a little bit now that she was single, but Max was cramping her style. What could I do?

"Danja, Ben and I are gypsies. We are traveling constantly around the world for his work. We cannot have the responsibility of a dog. It's hard enough taking care of ourselves—all of the flying, hotels, luggage, always in a new city or a new country—we cannot take Max, too. Ben is completely against the idea. He already said 'no' more than once."

To cheer her up, I did offer to come by a few afternoons a week to pick up Max for some nice long walks in the park.

"Afternoons in the park are not the solution, Mommy. I need to find a family or a kind person to take her."

It broke my heart to think of Max with a stranger, but I knew I could not bring her home.

When I arrived to pick up Max for our first afternoon walk together, I was delighted to hear her already barking for me when I got off the elevator. She remembered me! We walked first along lively Central Park South, past all the tourists and handsome cabs with their horses, but instead of going into the park, we cut right over to Park Avenue and headed uptown. Max was pulling me along like one of the horses pulling a carriage through the park.

It wasn't too long before a lovely lady approached us and said, "Oh, what a beautiful dog. This is my children's dream dog."

"Thank you. This is Max. She is my daughter's dog, and unfortunately, my daughter is thinking of finding a new home for her."

The lady quickly called her two children over and asked, "May we pet her?"

"Careful."

"Oh, they know. We had two dogs like this in France. Does your daughter really want to give her up?"

"Sadly, yes."

"We would take her immediately, and I would pay you. I know she is worth a lot, and we have a very large, thirteen-room apartment. She would have the life of a princess with us. I promise."

"That's very sweet. I will tell my daughter. Unfortunately, it's not my decision to make, but if you would kindly give me your name and telephone number, we will phone you."

Already, in just one hour, I had found a new home for Max. Walking the few blocks back to our apartment with her on one hand and the kind lady's phone number in the other, I was not happy.

I passed our doorman without even saying hello. When I opened the door to the apartment, Ben was sitting, like always, in his favorite chair, reading his *New York Times*. He looked up and saw that I was crying. "What's wrong?" he asked.

"I have Max here, Ben."

"Yeah, so? And why are you crying?"

"Danja doesn't want Max anymore. She asked me to help find another home for her. And already between her house and ours, I met a nice lady with children and a big home who wants to buy her. She is waiting to hear from us. It breaks my heart, Ben."

He slowly lowered his newspaper and looked at me with his big brown eyes. "A price tag on our dog? *Never*. You want her? You can have her."

"Really Ben, you mean it?" I couldn't believe my ears. What a surprise! I kissed Ben, full of joy. I kissed Max and danced with her around the apartment. I immediately phoned Danja at work.

"Danja, I've found a home for Max. I think she'll be very happy. And the best news is, I'm not a grandmother anymore! Now I'm a young mother again."

And so, like Ben predicted when we first saw Max, "that dog" was now "our dog."

Meet Maxi

I HAD NEVER seen Danja move so quickly. She arrived in less than an hour with all of Max's belongings, and together, we set about making our new family member feel at home on Madison Avenue. We put down wee-wee paper, found a place for Max to dine each day, and put a basket full of toys on the floor for her to choose from. Soon she was squeaking, barking, and running around all over the house playing with her rubber balls.

"Jesus Christ, Elke, is this our new life?" Ben scowled, which only made Max bark louder.

"Max, shhhh. Please. Behave yourself. Take it easy," I said.

Ben barked back, "Is she always this loud, Danja? Please."

"No, she's just excited. It's only the first day. She's not used to having so much room to play; remember she's been living in a shoe box."

Max continued to race around the apartment like a professional soccer player chasing her ball everywhere and barking at everything

in her path—every chair, every pillow, every table leg—everything. Even I must admit, it was a lot. I looked at Danja with a doubtful face, full of concern. "Holy canoli, Danja. Do you think she will ever calm down?"

"Yes, Mommy. She'll be fine. Relax."

Ben got up and went not so quietly into his den—competing with Max's barking by closing the door with a firm slam.

I could tell we might be in trouble. Was this how she behaved normally? Still, I pressed on as if everything would work out, hoping Ben would soon love Max like I already did.

"Mommy, don't forget, in the morning she eats at seven and the same at night, seven. Please always have fresh water, and on Sunday, she gets champagne."

"*Champagne?*"

"Not really, Mommy. I was kidding."

"I know, Danja. But red wine is okay, yes, with a plate of pasta? This is an Italian household after all."

We laughed. Max had joined us in the dining room by now, and while we discussed her daily routine, she found her way on to my lap. Looking down at her sweet, sleepy face, I knew everything would be okay.

"No pork ever, once a week an egg for her fur, and she loves baby carrots," Danja continued. "Here and there you can give her a little chicken and cottage cheese. Actually Mommy, she eats the same things you eat. But not too many people-food treats—this breed has to stay slim because of their long backs. Just like you, keep her lean and mean."

"I don't feel so lean today. Good-bye, *mein kind*. Thank you for the most beautiful gift. You can come and visit your sister anytime."

I gave Danja and Max a private moment to say their good-byes. I knew even though Danja wanted to give Max away that it would not be so easy. I heard from where I was in the living room the familiar "I love you, I love you, I love you." And Max's excited reply: "I love you, I love you, I love you too." I smiled and hoped that one day Max would say those words to me and Ben.

"Mommy, one more thing, keep your bathroom door closed and Ben's too. Max likes to bury her ball under the bathmat and chew her way through to it—leaving a shredded mess of a rug."

And I must say, Danja was right. I can't tell you how many bathmats I have replaced at friends' homes—in every color. And while Ben often forgets, I do try to keep the bathroom doors closed at home—even so, I find myself often at Bed Bath & Beyond. In fact, Maxi is shredding away at a beautiful bathmat as I write these pages. I guess I'll never learn.

After some kisses from both of us, Danja stepped into the elevator and placed Max in my arms. I told Danja that she should feel free to phone Max anytime—even collect.

I had a happy but heavy heart. I was thrilled with my new daughter but concerned that it might not be as easy for Danja without Max as she thought. I hoped we hadn't made this decision too quickly.

Going back inside with Max in my arms, I felt more at home than ever before. Ben and I never had a child together, but I had always secretly hoped for another addition to our family. Finally, here she was. I felt complete.

Now I needed to work on Ben. I went straight to his den and knocked on the door with a bang so that he would hear me over his evening news, which he watches so loudly that you would think he was deaf.

"Ben, please, it's so loud. Have you gone crazy?"

"I was trying to hear over the dog's barking."

"This is not a dog. This is Max. She's our baby." And with that, I put Max on her new daddy's lap. She gave him a mouthful of wet kisses right away. He quickly turned the sound down on the television as if protecting her sensitive ears from the noise, and they cozied up together as I went to the kitchen to prepare dinner.

So far it was all going smoothly. Max stayed with Ben the whole time I cooked. After preparing our meal, I filled Max's bowl with dry food and got her some fresh water for our first family meal together.

"Dinner is served."

Max ran in, easily beating Ben to the table. She couldn't wait to dig in. It felt wonderful to have such youthful enthusiasm in the house. I haven't seen Ben run in many years.

I had made an extra effort to prepare the best meal of the week, pasta Sicilian style, some of Ben's beloved homemade Italian sausages, a big fresh salad, and of course a nice bottle of red wine. To give it a romantic touch, I also lit some candles and put on DeStefano singing Ben's favorite Italian arias softly in the background.

After Max finished her meal in the kitchen, she joined us for some of ours in the dining room. Pulling a string of pasta from his plate with a sheepish grin, Ben asked, "Do you think she likes pasta?"

"Ben, please, don't start."

And like a child, Ben rose and put the string of pasta in Max's bowl, singing sweetly, "Maxi, Maxi. Mangia, Mangia."

Max immediately ran to her bowl and slurped up the pasta like a vacuum cleaner. "Well, I guess Maxi likes your cooking."

"Basta, Ben. No more pasta. Please. Soon you'll be giving her wine. And her name is Max, not Maxi."

"First of all, if she's gonna be my dog, she's gonna eat pasta. And second, who is Max? She's a little girl. I'm calling her Maxi. You can call her what you want."

"You know, you are right. She is a beautiful little girl." And so, Max became Maxi.

Maxi Becomes a *Real* New Yorker

*I*T DIDN'T TAKE long for reality to set in. How would we possibly fit Maxi into our lifestyle? Dogs are not historically welcome in the New York City nightlife, and we went out almost every night. And how about traveling? Would Maxi be able to join us on our trips around the world?

This could be more difficult than I had originally thought. I could only hope that our next on-location destination would be in a dog-friendly country—perhaps Germany or France. God forbid the next picture would shoot in England. What would we do?

"Ben, what will happen with Maxi tomorrow night?" Our friends the Weisslers had invited us to the opening night of *Annie Get Your Gun*, which they were producing on Broadway with Bernadette Peters. It was a very big event.

"What did Danja do when she went out?"

"She left her locked up in the kitchen."

"So? Here she has the whole apartment. We'll put on some music and she'll be fine. What's the problem?"

"Better may be the large bathroom. We can close her in there with her ball, her blanket, and her food and water."

That afternoon we went to Petco and bought a fence that was nearly four feet tall to keep Maxi in Ben's bathroom. Even the lady at the store commented that we didn't need such a tall fence for such a little dog. But I wanted to be safe.

We prepared the space lovingly. Frank Sinatra and Andrea Bocelli would serenade her for the few hours while we were away.

I was already nervous. How would this little girl do alone? Would she hurt herself? Would she hurt our home? What if a pipe broke? We had suffered through several floods recently.

I was having second thoughts about leaving. But Ben pulled me impatiently out of the apartment and said, "She will be fine. Let's go."

I gave Maxi a last look and waved good-bye. She looked at me with her beautiful sad, brown eyes as if to say, "Where are you going? Don't leave me alone." She already knew how to pull on my heartstrings.

During the entire happy musical, Maxi was on my mind. The two and a half hours felt like three days. I couldn't stop thinking about my baby home all alone.

When we finally arrived back at our apartment, I was anxious to see how Maxi was doing. We opened the door and there she was, not in the bathroom where we'd left her, but right there. Delighted to see us, she barked and jumped on us, and I thought her tail might wag off from overexcitement. Somehow that little dog had climbed over our four-foot-high fence.

Ben smiled at her with such pride. "Now this is what I call a dog."

"How did she do that?" I asked.

"She's a genius," Ben said. "That's because she has the blood of a hunting dog, and from tomorrow on, no more fence. She can have the whole apartment. I trust her. Do you trust her?"

The bathroom and the apartment were impeccable. Not one thing was out of order. She had arranged her potty perfectly on the paper and her ball swam in her water bowl.

"Yes I do," I said. But I didn't really. There were about a thousand potential targets in our home for an excited dog to destroy.

THE NEXT EVENING Ben said, "I want to prove to you this dog will not do anything bad. She's a genius."

"Ben, I don't think so."

"Let's experiment."

And so, we left her alone for the evening loose in the apartment with music, balls, and food. When we arrived home, she was waiting for us by the door just like the night before.

"Didn't I tell you? She's a genius," Ben said.

Maxi looked at us triumphantly as if to say, "I'd like to show you something, come with me." She turned around and led us to one of our couches that had been recently re-covered in a beautiful cognac silk.

I followed her through the living room to the couch, and I couldn't believe my eyes. Maxi had peed all over it.

"Holy Christ, Ben. This is your genius?"

And Maxi has never been left alone since.

LUCKILY, THE NEXT couple of nights were spent in restaurants where we knew the owners. Maxi sat silently in her bag under the table and behaved like a princess. No complaints. No one even knew she was there.

From then on, it was almost like Ben enjoyed taking Maxi with us everywhere—no matter how big the hurdle getting her inside. To this day, I think he secretly enjoys the challenge. Maxi must have liked coming along, too. One of those first nights, on our way to a dinner party, we called her and called her, but she was nowhere to be found. She didn't come running through the house ready to go. We offered treats . . . nothing. Finally, out of the corner of my eye, I saw her bag move and her little head popped out; she was already ready to go, waiting for us. We melted like ice cream in the sun.

From then on, Maxi watched us like a hawk; always alert. When she saw me getting ready, that was her signal—she was already in her bag prepared to go long before I took my curlers out.

It was the holiday season in New York City. Night after night we painted the town—Ben, Maxi, and me. We wined and dined at Le Cirque, Bravo Gianni, Cipriani, La Goulue, Gino, The Boat House, Primola, Nello, Centolira, and Mellon's. Maxi even joined us under Sonny Grosso's table at Rao's in East Harlem where mobsters drink with policemen and Park Avenue players dine with gangsters, lawyers, and the occasional judge—*people* wait sometimes for two years to get in for dinner, but not Maxi. The owner's wife Anne liked Maxi so much that some time before she passed away she gave me her private recipe for Maxi's favorite lemon chicken. I like to call it "connected chicken."

I remember once going to a tiny French restaurant. We gave up our coats and the maître d asked, "Monsieur Gazzara, may I take your bag?"

Ben said, "Oh, no, no, no, I'll keep it. I have all my money in here."

A little while later, during dinner, our waiter stepped a little too

close to the bag resting near Ben's feet under the table and Maxi spoke up, loudly.

At that very moment, the maître d passed by our table and said with a knowing look, "Monsieur Gazzara, your money is barking."

When people ask for restaurant recommendations, I think Maxi could answer as well as I could. Even though no New York restaurant officially allows dogs, Maxi certainly knows where to go; we have smuggled her in everywhere like a German refugee. And my daughter Danja was right—Maxi and I do eat the same things, mostly chicken and often in restaurants. She gets a little under the table while I eat on top. And I always accept with pleasure a doggie bag for our little girl.

ANOTHER BEAUTIFUL RITUAL began in those early days—Maxi's bath. Dachshunds are not known for being big swimmers; in fact, they don't like water at all. After some failed attempts in the bathtub where she would panic and splash and even eat the soap, drenching me in the process, Ben decided he would take her in the shower with him, but he needed my assistance. Step by step—Ben got in first and warmed up the water. I put Maxi in his arms and prepared the dog shampoo. She seemed to love it right away when she got my special massaging treatment; she must have felt like she was at a spa. Ben held her gently while I bathed her, and then he lovingly rinsed her with the

warm shower water before carefully placing her in my towel-covered arms like a proud father handing off his freshly bathed newborn baby back to mama. Toweling her off, my work continued—I carefully cleaned her ears, brushed her teeth, and, like a silly mother, sang her a lullaby to keep her calm through the whole experience. Maxi took as much pampering as she could, and then all of a sudden, she jumped from my lap and bolted from the bathroom like a torpedo. When I caught up to her, she shook herself, sending water all over me. I wished I had worn a raincoat.

It was very special to have this dog in our lives suddenly. I loved watching Ben fall in love with her. I loved falling in love with her myself. Maxi quickly became the apple of our eyes. We found ourselves walking the streets of the city more than ever. Central Park, only one block from our home, became our backyard for the first time in our many years living on Madison Avenue. Neighbors and strangers alike with dogs were suddenly friends and acquaintances in our daily routine. With Maxi by our side, unexpected conversations occurred more than ever. I've found that I enjoy talking to other dog owners, hearing their stories—positive and negative—and discovering that there is something special in every dog-owner relationship.

Even more unexpected, though, was discovering Maxi's appeal to the opposite sex. Women followed Ben and men followed me—all because of Maxi. Some must have been half our age, but they followed nonetheless. It was charming.

After being married for so long, I had forgotten some of the silly pick-up lines men often use. One Saturday afternoon, near the steps of the Metropolitan Museum of Art, Maxi and I were approached by a very handsome man. He looked at me and then he looked at Maxi and asked, "What kind of dog is that?"

"It's a lion," I said playfully.

"What's your lion's name?"

"Her name is Maxi."

"How old is Maxi?"

"She's my age. Seven."

"And where does Maxi live?" he asked flirtatiously.

"Maxi lives on Madison Avenue with me . . ." and even though I was amused and hated to spoil the fun, I continued, "and my husband."

"He's a very lucky man."

And that was that. Home we went to our lucky man.

Perhaps a week later, another young man found Maxi and me walking in Central Park. He said, "Miss, do you know your dog favors the left leg in the back? It looks like she has a small limp."

"It's not true," I said.

"You can't see because she's right beside you. I'll prove it to you, give me the leash and we'll walk in front of you."

"Never," I said, "no, never."

"Are you afraid I'll steal your dog?"

"Maybe," I said with a laugh.

He also laughed and then went on his way.

That same afternoon, on our way to a late lunch, watching Ben and Maxi walk ahead of me, I couldn't believe my eyes. That stranger was right. Maxi does have a crooked swagger, and funny enough, so does Ben. I guess it runs in the family.

THAT YEAR, WE took our first official family photo in front of our Christmas tree and every decoration on that tree was a dachshund. Maxi even had her own stocking. We had only been together just over a month, but somehow, I couldn't remember life before Maxi.

The Christmas days were beautiful. Friends and family joined us and showered Maxi with adorable toys and gifts and treats. It really was like having a little girl. We had such fun. Danja brought Maxi a red velvet collar with gold bells and a pair of reindeer antlers. Maxi was so excited to see her that she made a pee-pee the instant Danja came in the door. They kissed and spoke their "I love yous." All night long, Maxi would bring her balls and toys to Danja. They played together, and I could see how much they still loved each other.

"How is it going with Max, Mommy? Are you having a good time?"

"We love her so much. I can't thank you enough for this precious present, perhaps the best present I ever got."

"She has it very good here. In my next life, I would like to be a dog in your house," Danja joked.

"Your life was not so bad either, *mein kind*."

"Maybe you should get another dog so Max can have a sister or a brother. It's not always fun growing up a single child. You know what I mean, Mommy."

"You were more than plenty for me, Danja, and so is Maxi."

But somehow I felt awkward.

I know I made a lot of mistakes as a young mother. I wasn't always able to take Danja with me everywhere because of my work. As a model, I traveled frequently, often for weeks and in locales that were not ideal for children. After my divorce, for some years during her early childhood, Danja lived with her father in South Africa. I felt then and now that Danja resented me for that. Our relationship was sometimes troubled. Adopting my daughter's dog somehow gave me a second chance at motherhood, at least in my mind; and now I could take my new daughter everywhere.

I wish I could have taken Danja everywhere, too.

Happy Birthday to Me

I LOVE BIRTHDAYS, and I was really looking forward to sharing my special evening that year with my husband, my daughter, my dog, and a few good friends. Maxi was dressed to the nines for the party and so was I. To celebrate, I had bought a new outfit to match a stunning necklace Ben had surprised me with, and Maxi was wearing a big matching bow around her neck like Madame Butterfly.

Walking down the long, narrow stairway into Oba, a very popular and very loud nightclub in New York, Maxi popped her little head out of her bag when she heard all of the noise as if she were asking, "Where are you taking me?" I stopped, reached in my pocket and pulled out a tissue, tore it in half, rolled the pieces up in a ball, and put them in Maxi's ears—earplugs.

Ben looked at me and said, "I wish you could stuff my ears, too."

We continued down the stairs and entered the noisy club. We walked toward the table where my friends and Danja were already sitting. They had champagne waiting and quickly poured a glass for Ben and me. We put Maxi's bag between us in the booth. She seemed comfortable; in fact, she fell asleep.

The most delicious dinner was served. We had a feast and the pink heart-shaped birthday cake was a dream. I blew out the one candle with a loud laugh realizing I already had my most precious birthday wish with me, sleeping soundly in her bag. Everybody near us applauded, then suddenly Brazilian music blared from every loud speaker. Ben stood up and said, "Let's dance, birthday girl."

Nothing could have made me happier. I jumped on my heels, took Ben's hand, and we started to samba. Like always, Ben was ready to give up after the first dance, but I kept him on the dance floor for at least another song or two. As we returned to the table, we saw our little Maxi sitting on Danja's lap. Our friends poured more champagne for all of us and I noticed that my daughter was losing control a little bit. She got up and said, "Now I'm going to dance with Maxi."

Ben said, "Don't do that, it's too noisy out there for her."

"I do what I want with my dog," Danja replied curtly.

"Wait a moment, Danja," I said. "Isn't Maxi our dog now?"

"No. I decided to take her back."

I was speechless. My body went numb.

"You've got to be kidding," Ben said.

"No, I'm not. I want my dog back. Get your own dog." With that she marched to the dance floor with Maxi in her arms. I couldn't hold back my tears. Was this really happening?

Ben said, "Don't worry. She's tipsy."

A few songs later, Danja and Maxi returned from the dance floor. She could tell that I had been crying but didn't seem to care. She had another drink, and things really began to get out of hand.

At some point, during the exchange of some harsh words, Danja, with one of her overly dramatic gestures, struck Ben right in the face. Well, there it started.

Ben snapped. The two of them made quite a scene. It wasn't a pretty picture, but no one was hurt, thank God, except for our pride. I was stunned. What a nightmare. What an embarrassment. What a birthday.

"LET'S GO HOME," Ben said firmly.

Almost paralyzed and with a heavy heart, I climbed the long, narrow staircase one step after the other—the very same steps I had just come down with such joy and happiness—only this time, sadly, without either of my daughters.

When we got into the taxi, Ben said to me right away, "You know, I'm not sure she meant to hit me; I think it might have been an accident. But I couldn't help myself. I was protecting you."

I simply said, "It's okay Ben. Let's go home." And without Maxi, we rode silently back to our apartment.

Ben and Danja had always had a turbulent relationship. And here it was again. But this time, it had come to blows, and I wasn't sure it could be repaired. As always, my heart was torn between these two loves of my life—only now there were three loves, and I was going home with only one. My heart ached immensely.

When we entered the apartment, I knew it would not be the same without Maxi. I walked to the kitchen and looked down at her bowls where she eats and drinks; in the living room, I saw the cushion she rests on—but when I went into the bedroom and saw her little bed where she slept very near to our bed, I broke down and really cried. After only two months of having Maxi, I couldn't bear to see all of her belongings now. I went immediately to bed to lie down.

"I'll get you another dog tomorrow," Ben said. "Please try to get some rest. I'm sorry about tonight. I'm sorry for you."

I knew he was sorry for me, but he was also sorry for Maxi. I could see, too, that Ben was trying to hide his disappointment. Maxi had conquered his heart as well.

Hoping to get over the night and wake up from this terrible dream, we went to bed and tried unsuccessfully to sleep. Ben was up and down all night—I tossed and turned endlessly. Sometime just before dawn, I must have finally found deep sleep because I was awakened suddenly with little wet kisses. I knew it couldn't be Ben. Maxi was home.

Early in the morning, with what must have been a horrible hangover, Danja had come to her senses. She arrived unannounced and put Maxi in our elevator. Ben received a call from our concierge that "someone special" was on the way up.

When Maxi appeared, I swooped her up in my arms and did not stop kissing her. She was home. She was ours again.

Maxi in Italy

*M*AMMA MIA, OFF to Italy. Maxi's first flight. I have to admit I was very nervous. The flight from New York to Rome is nearly nine hours. With car travel, luggage handling, and checking in, by the time we arrive at our home in Umbria, it's nearly twelve hours later. I was very concerned about Maxi's little bladder. It would be a long time to spend in that bag. Could she do it? We had heard that some dogs get very nervous and agitated when they travel. Some cry, some suffer from motion sickness, and some even throw up.

Packing is a full-time job in our house. We always plan to travel light, but we end up packing as if we were going to spend a year overseas, in some strange place, when in fact we are simply going from our New York home to our Italian home. Making sure she wouldn't be left behind, Maxi had smuggled herself into Ben's suitcase. When I came back into the room to gather some final things, she popped up between

Ben's underwear and socks. I laughed out loud and she joined me with her rousing bark. We were ready for takeoff.

"Ben, what do you think? Should we give Maxi a little bit of Valium or maybe a sip of beer like they gave babies in Germany to calm them down?"

"No, my dog doesn't drink. She will fly on the natch."

I was well prepared. I had packed meals, treats, toys, potty paper, and, most importantly, Maxi's health certificates. Ben, who was also nervous about Maxi's first flight, must have asked me five times if I had those certificates.

After our luggage was checked by airport security, I took Maxi in my arms and walked her through the metal detectors. Everything went smoothly. We had a relaxing hour in the VIP lounge where Maxi entertained the other waiting passengers by occasionally popping her little head out to say hello. She was an instant star, and how happy we were to be her proud parents.

With Maxi safely in her bag, we boarded the plane. Ben and I put her carefully between our feet. She was asleep before takeoff. She slept through our cocktail hour, but as soon as the rubber chicken arrived, her bag began to shake. Maxi wiggled her way out for dinner. We gave her a few bites, continuing to spoil her. Now every time we fly, Maxi is our dinner date.

She and Ben both fell asleep as soon as dinner was finished. And both of them snored. Holy canoli! I couldn't believe it. What noises they made. No doubt she's Ben's daughter.

Five hours into the flight, the stewardess politely approached me and said, "Mrs. Gazzara, my list says that you have a dog with you. But obviously they made a mistake. I have not seen a dog the entire trip."

"No mistake," I said, looking toward Ben. "The dog is sleeping."

She looked over to Ben with a funny expression. I laughed and pointed to Maxi's bag on the floor. The stewardess and I giggled quietly together. She looked down and said, "That is the best behaved dog I have ever flown with."

During the flight, Maxi occasionally peeked out to make sure we were still there. Even when I picked her up carefully, hiding her under my blanket, and placed her in my lap, all she wanted to do was return to her bag. It was her home. She felt safe there. I turned to Ben and said, "I think we have a frequent flyer on our hands."

The rest of the plane ride was a breeze. Maxi passed with flying colors. She even made a pee-pee in the toilet of the airplane after I laid down some newspaper for her to use. What a good girl.

Once we landed, I took Maxi outside the airport while Ben waited inside for our luggage. It worked like a charm. When she had finished her business, I brought her close to me and hugged her, "*Benvenuta in bell'Italia*," I said.

The hour-and-forty-five-minute journey from the airport in Rome to our home in Umbria is filled with beauty. In the spring and summer, the fields of golden sunflowers there might have inspired Van Gogh. Driving in the early morning hours through the medieval villages, the smell of freshly baked bread mixes with the sweet aromas of fruits and spices, and that is always a delight. We stopped for a second breakfast. The baked pork (*porchetta*) is a favorite of ours. Before we bit into it, we found a raw carrot for Maxi to munch on. Maxi was especially happy; it was her first Italian carrot, and Italian carrots are sweet and tasty. Maxi agreed: It was gone in two seconds.

AS WE STROLLED through the narrow village streets, Maxi was soon the center of attention. She offered kisses to the villagers who welcomed her. "*Buon giorno, amore,*" they said. Maxi was on top of the world and already felt right at home.

The last few minutes of the drive home are perhaps the most spectacular. The winding roads and breathtaking views of the snow-capped Apennine Mountains lead straight to our house, which we call Casa Bali. The gated drive is lined with stunning pine trees standing like candles in line while our home is surrounded by ancient olive trees and many wonderful flowers, including roses, jasmine, and lavender. It was a perfect day. The sun was shining. The clouds were passing gently by and the scent from the flowers was everywhere. When we got out of the car, Maxi headed right to the pool area and we followed, not taking the luggage out or opening the house. It was clear she was in search of something. She found a private patch of lavender to make her permanent powder room. And like a good hunting dog, she checked out her territory. Looking up, I saw in the distance one of my most beloved views in the whole world, the castle in the clouds. There is nothing else to see here. Nothing blocks our view, no neighbors, no noises, nothing. We have only these beautiful old trees, the vibrant and fragrant flowers, the many colors of Casa Bali, and this ancient castle, on a far away hill, nestled in the clouds. Casa Bali is our *piccolo paradiso*.

Some years ago, just after Ben and I were married, we spent a few months on the island of Bali. Ben was working on a picture there called *Beyond the Ocean*. We were enchanted immediately with the island's charm, customs, people, and gorgeous scenery. Not knowing if we would ever return, I decided to take some of Bali with us. While Ben was shooting, I spent my days and some nights leisurely wandering the island and purchasing their magnificent, handcrafted furniture and stunning, colorful artwork for our home in Italy that was still being built. We had decided to create a second home in Umbria because Ben worked often in Europe and I thought it would be a good idea to bring him back to his Italian roots.

By the time Ben's picture wrapped, we had five and a half large containers of Bali to take back to Italy with us. For Ben, I bought a lifetime supply of bathing suits, sarongs, and shirts, and for me, I bought the same plus dresses, skirts, jewelry, and shoes—everything in every color. Even today we stick to the customs we started all those years ago—we both wear our multicolored batik prints and comfortable Balinese attire whenever we are home at Casa Bali. I also wear a lovely wreath of flowers in my hair when I am there. It has actually become my trademark. I also bought loads of antique fabrics to cover couches and make curtains for years to come.

AND NOW, WHAT a joy it was to share this little paradise in Umbria that we call Casa Bali with our adorable little Maxi. There were plenty of pleasures here for her—from the overstuffed pillows to Ben's large, comfortable opium bed that she would make her very own private palace—Casa Bali is the perfect place for a little princess like Maxi.

AFTER LIVING IN Italy for many years now and being married to an Italian, I almost feel Italian myself. Watching Maxi run through the olive trees chasing rabbits and birds—I knew she would soon feel like an Italian too. I said to Ben, "Look at how Maxi jumps around after twelve hours of traveling. She must have no jet lag at all."

"Neither do I," Ben said.

Boy I did! Traveling to and from Europe hits me for a week on both sides; it really wipes me out. Ben always tells me to stay awake until bedtime, but often, by lunchtime, I'm already so sleepy that I could fall with my face in my pasta. I wish I had Maxi's energy.

While Ben and I enjoyed a nice lunch on our terrace, Maxi played in the vineyard below, apparently trying to determine the difference between the red and white grapes. She nosed around like a pig digging for truffles and made herself right at home, eventually lying down on the warm terra cotta, basking in the sun between the large stone-carved statues of the king and queen of Bali.

I was reminded of a charming conversation I had with one of the Balinese actors in the movie with Ben so many moons ago. Like many tropical islands, Bali is paradise-warm during the day and often a bit chilly at night. Every night, coming and going from our hotel, we saw packs and packs of wild dogs resting on the warm soil streets. I don't know where they must have hidden during the day because I never saw them except at night. I had to carry a flashlight not to step on them; they were packed so tightly on the streets. Out of sheer curiosity, I asked this young Balinese actor, "What is it in Bali with dogs? It seems like they are not appreciated or respected at all here."

"It's because they eat the offerings."

I looked at him even more curiously.

He explained, "You know, the regular offerings that the Hindus make to God. Often they contain rice, flowers, fruits, and sometimes vegetables. The people here have lost respect for dogs because they not only destroy the beautiful ornaments, but they also devour the offerings."

"Funny, I never thought of that. Who else would eat it?"

"Well it's meant for God to eat. My whole life, I always found it interesting that the offerings are made for God and often eaten by a dog, until one day I had an awakening—dog spelled backwards *is* God. God was getting those offerings all along."

I will never forget that conversation.

AFTER LUNCH, I made a flower collar for Maxi with wild flowers and lavender like I had seen in Bali. The three of us looked like quite the royal family. And while she *was* adorable in her flowers, I'm sure, if given the chance, she would have joined those wild pack dogs in Bali. I think I'll have to carefully keep track of the offerings here; not too many of God's stolen gifts for this dog.

THE MYSTICAL TWILIGHT hours came and went that first evening, and it was finally time for a good night's sleep. In Casa Bali, Ben and I each have a private wing, so for the first time since we adopted Maxi, we would have to figure out who would get to sleep with her. We decided to make a game of it. When it was time for bed, we put Maxi in the den between the two of us. Ben went his way and I went mine. We caught each other peeking around the sides of our doors to see which direction Maxi would go, but she just sat in the center of the den looking from Ben to me and back as if we were completely bananas.

And then Ben broke the rules. He began calling, "Maxi, I love you, come to daddy."

Not to be outdone, I joined in, "Maxi, Maxi, I love you," when suddenly my eyes caught sight of a stuffed koala bear sitting nearby on my bookshelf. I grabbed it and tossed it a few feet in front of me. Maxi took the bait. Pouncing on the koala like a lion's prey, she ran to me and we spent the rest of the night together.

Maxi and I both slept long and peacefully. When we woke up the next morning, the koala bear, half un-stuffed, was still lying between us like a fresh night's kill. Ben brought in a nice tray of coffee and fresh Italian cornetto when he heard us moving around. In Italy, he is always up hours before me. He goes to the village very early to have his coffee and to pick up the *Herald Tribune*. Forever the romantic, Ben often spoils me there with breakfast in bed.

"I missed my girl last night. My feelings are hurt."

"Which girl, Ben?"

"Who do you think?"

"You missed Maxi," I guessed.

"I missed you both."

But I knew he missed Maxi. "Cheer up Ben; tonight, Maxi will be with you."

"You promise?"

"You silly Sicilian, I promise."

And ever since, Maxi alternately enjoys sleeping with Ben or sleeping with me when we are at Casa Bali.

That next night, Maxi gave Ben quite a treat. We had entertained some friends with a nice dinner grilled outside. There was pasta, foccacia, chicken, steak, salad, sausage—you name it—and as always plenty of wine. Maxi stayed near the grill hoping Franca, our cook, would drop some meat. She may have had a little luck there, but she helped herself to a whole lot of trouble in the trash. She must have eaten enough for a lifetime. Her belly was so swollen she looked like a little stuffed pig. When it was finally bedtime, Ben placed Maxi carefully in a nest of blankets and towels on his bed in case of an accident and to make her as comfortable as possible. She slept the entire night on her back snoring like a drunken sailor. Poor Ben, I don't think he slept at all.

The next morning, he brought Maxi to my room and said, "Jesus Christ, you never heard a dog snore like this."

"Ben, I've been hearing it for twenty years. Sound familiar?"

Maxi was sick for three days. Worried, we phoned our vet in New York whose only advice was to watch her closely, be sure she drank plenty of water, and wait for her to eliminate. It was hard to stand by and watch her suffer. But our vet was right and what an elimination!

Old dog, new tricks—new dog, old tricks—Maxi never learned this lesson. To this day she is a thief. She will steal food any chance she gets. Only one week later, she got sick again after eating a lot of uncooked sausage from the garbage. This time she had to suffer even more. She threw up and had bad bowels for days. We learned our lesson though—Maxi must be allergic to *schwein* (that's pork in German).

"Maybe she's Jewish," Ben said.

"Or Muslim," I said.

"I think she learned her lesson," Ben laughed.

"Don't be so sure."

Roma

Arrivederci Umbria, *Buon giorno bella* Roma! Even though we still had a few weeks before shooting was to begin on Ben's film, *No Man's Land*, we had to go to Rome for a costume fitting and some meetings. Fortunately, we found out that our favorite hotel, the Hotel De La Ville, on top of the Piazza Di Spagna, would accept Maxi. Not only did they accept her, but they gave us our special suite with an enormous terrace overlooking the entire Eternal City. Ben and I have been enjoying the Hotel De La Ville since we first met some twenty-five years ago. We even lived there once in sin before we were married.

I met Ben during the filming of *Inchon* in Seoul, Korea, where they shot the exteriors of the film that starred Lawrence Olivier, Jacqueline Bisset, David Janssen, Toshirô Mifune, and our friend Rex Reed. I was there producing a documentary on the making of *Inchon*. My daughter Danja, who was only eight years old at the time, was with me too. Actually, it was Danja who introduced me to Ben for the first time

after she met him in an elevator and thought he might be perfect for me. Twenty-five years later, I guess she was right. After Korea, the entire cast and crew flew to Rome for interior shots.

EVEN AFTER ALL of these years, when we enter the grand lobby of the Hotel De La Ville, we are greeted by the staff with open arms and smiling faces. Actually, everywhere we go in Italy we are welcomed like family because Italy loves Ben and Ben loves Italy. He made his first film there with Toto and Anna Magnani when he was in his twenties and has since appeared in dozens of Italian movies.

When we arrived at the hotel, this time was no different. There was a lot of commotion with many hugs from the staff. With dramatic flair, Ben reached inside the bag and pulled Maxi out, placing her on the marble desk, announcing, "This is the *other* love of my life. Meet Maxi."

"She's really beautiful. I have her sisters at home in Pasadena," an elegant American lady said as she approached us.

"Aren't they the smartest dogs in the world?" I asked.

"Not only the smartest, but also the best," the lovely lady said. "My name is Lupe Atwood."

She and I became friends right there, and we still are. Maxi brought us together.

Right away when we entered our favorite suite, Ben threw open the French doors to the terrace and tossed Maxi's squeaky ball outside. She was in heaven playing with that ball all around the large terra cotta flower pots filled with geraniums and lavender.

The next day, we joined Maxi outside on the terrace to take some sun. I was lying in a colorful bikini working on my tan when I felt the first sting from that silent visitor. My ring finger started to burn and my hand swelled up like a muffin. But before I could even move to go back inside, I felt the second sting on my bottom. Suddenly, looking around, I noticed there were bees everywhere. I immediately got up to go inside and get dressed, announcing, "It looks like breakfast is over, Ben."

"Wait a minute. Sit down; I'll take care of it."

And did he. Ben went into the suite and gathered all of the tiny packages of honey from the breakfast tray and, opening them one by one, he placed them on the far wall of the terrace connected to the Hotel Hassler saying, "Done. Don't worry. They won't go near you. They'll be too busy eating."

I don't know what he was thinking or what he thought would happen, but the next thing I knew, I looked up and the bees had multiplied—they were everywhere. It looked like every bee in Rome came for a bite of Ben's honey. What a disaster. They were swarming and buzzing all around us. It could have been a scene from Hitchcock's *The Birds*. I've never seen or heard anything like that. I ran inside to escape the attack.

From behind the closed screen door, I said, "Ben, take care, take Maxi. I don't want her to get hurt."

Laughing, Ben said, "Bees don't bite dogs, only juicy women."

And that's when I saw Maxi chasing and biting and swallowing one bee after another. It was as though she were protecting me, angry that they had hurt me. She had come to my rescue.

I guess Ben was right. Maxi didn't get stung and neither did he. That must make me the sweet one.

Capri

BEN DECIDED TO reward me for his honey heroics with a weekend trip to a favorite island of ours—Capri. I have been going there since I was seventeen years old. There is no place on earth where the moon is more beautiful than in Capri. It is perhaps the island's only free luxury. That moon could be straight from the set of a movie, *luna Caprese*.

We arrived by boat from Napoli. The port was full of handsome, uniformed porters waiting to greet and receive the guests and take their luggage, which they would transport in their carts to the various hotels. We gave them everything but Maxi. In the midst of the pleasant confusion, I am always amazed that my luggage somehow turns up in my room before I do.

We took the famous taxi ride from *marina piccola*, the harbor, up the winding road along the seacoast full of orange and olive trees to nearby the piazzetta of Capri. Cars are not allowed past a certain point. With pleasure, Ben, Maxi, and I walked through to the piazza

where everyone arrives and departs with public fanfare—nobody goes unnoticed. With Maxi eagerly leading the way on her virgin visit—we drew even more attention. There are not many dogs in Capri. As small as she is, she still made quite a big splash.

We made our way through the charming village to the hotel Quissisana where I was once crowned Miss Capri. It seems like only yesterday that I was a skinny, awkward photo-model suddenly surprised with that crown. I am forever fond of the Italians for making a young country girl from Germany feel like a million dollars. Even though I have stayed there with Ben many nights since, each time I approach the exquisite landmark hotel, I still feel the butterflies from that night so long ago.

Immediately when we entered the lobby we were received by Mr. Morgano, the owner of the hotel. "*Buon giorno Signore e Signora Gazzara.*" But his bright smile and warm welcome quickly changed when he noticed Maxi. "Oh," he said, "I didn't know you were coming with a dog."

"Is that a problem?" Ben asked.

"Yes Signore. We don't allow dogs in the hotel. I am very sorry."

Those butterflies in my stomach became very nervous and agitated. I don't know what we were thinking—we hadn't thought to announce Maxi's arrival. Already we had forgotten we are three instead of two.

"What can we do, Mr. Morgano?" Ben asked. "Please, let's give it a try. She behaves better than most people I know."

Knowing this situation required extra charm, I said, "Mr. Morgano, of course you are the boss, but believe me, Maxi will not make any problems here—I guarantee you."

Thank goodness Mr. Morgano trusted us.

We found our luggage waiting for us in the most elegant suite with a balcony overlooking the Mediterranean and the Faraglione, two enormous rocks jutting out from the sea, Capri's trademark. Ben changed into a light linen outfit and off he went with Maxi to Tiberio in the piazza to have his campari and wait for me to join them for lunch.

The days and nights in Capri are always filled with long lunches, leisurely naps, luxurious dinners, and numerous nightcaps with music, laughs, and plenty of Italian romance. And these days and nights were no different. During our weekend excursion, Maxi strolled the carless streets without a leash, soaking up the warm Mediterranean sun with the best of the jet-setters.

It was during one of the long, languid Italian lunches in the lush, flowered garden of the hotel that I looked around and saw that Maxi had escaped from her carrying case and was nowhere to be seen.

"Ben, Maxi's gone!"

"Where did she go?"

"I don't know," I said.

"Don't worry," he assured me. "She can't have gone far."

"I'm going to track her down." And with that I left Ben at the table, calling Maxi's name over and over.

I walked through the garden and into a beautifully appointed empty salon that led to the large marble lobby. And there she was, little Maxi, pushing what looked like a white rubber ball toward an elderly man. She got the ball within five feet of him and gave it a strong final push with her nose, sending it to rest between the man's legs. He then took the ball and rolled it the length of the lobby and Maxi repeated her routine to the delight of members of the staff and a few of the clients but most especially the man she was playing with. I was stunned to see who that gentleman was.

"Mr. Morgano, please forgive us. I don't know how she got in here."

"Signora Gazzara, your dog is a marvel. She is welcome at the Quissisana hotel anytime."

I smiled appreciatively, picking up Maxi and the white ball she had been playing with, which turned out not to be a ball at all, but a firm, round piece of mozzarella cheese that Maxi had obviously lifted from our low garden table and then made a fast break for the interior of the hotel. At some point, she must have decided that before she ate the cheese, she would play with it. As Mr. Morgano tenderly caressed her head and neck, he said, "This is the most intelligent dog I've ever seen."

No mother ever smiled more proudly. When I returned to lunch with Ben, I got rid of the old, beaten-up piece of mozzarella and I ordered her a fresh clean one that she looked at for a long time as though trying to decide again, "Should I eat it or should I play with it?"

She ate it.

Holland

W E ARRIVED IN Holland on a gray, misty morning. After flying all night from New York, we were anxious to get to our hotel and settle in for our six-week stay. There was a kind man from India waiting to help us with our luggage and drive us to the location of Ben's next film. He was unfortunately afraid of dogs, even our little Maxi, and on top of that, he informed us that he was not feeling well.

Uh oh, not a good start in Holland.

"How far is the hotel, Ben?"

"It can't be that far," Ben said, "ask the driver."

"Sir, excuse me, how far are we going?" I asked.

"Three or three and a half hours. Depends on the rain."

"Are you sure?"

"Yes. About three hours," he replied. "We have to go to the other side of Holland, close to the German border, to a tiny village with no airport."

"Let's burn rubber," Ben said.

And off we went with a sick driver who was afraid of Maxi and too tired to be in charge of our lives for the next several rainy hours. This man was a mess. We had to pull the car over several times so he could vomit on the side of the road.

"He must be pregnant," I said to Ben, "this is morning sickness."

"Must have been a tough night."

After several stops and starts, the driver finally called in a replacement, which only added to an already too-long trip from New York. What should have been three and a half hours turned into what felt like an eternity.

But when we finally arrived at our destination, we were amazed. It was like arriving in Shangri-La or Camelot. Our hotel was an impeccable private villa that had been turned into a four-star hotel with five-star views of rolling, green meadows dotted with what looked like hundreds of white clouds that turned out to be sheep. What a sight. Our suite was large and luxurious. We would all be very comfortable here for the next six weeks. The staff was friendly, and soon, they all loved Maxi.

Ben's picture was called *Undertaker's Paradise*. It was a German comedy about a couple of young guys who started a funeral parlor in a town where no one died. I don't normally join Ben when he is on the set, so during those rainy days in Holland, I wandered the small town with Maxi for as many lunches and shopping trips as a woman and a dog can have in a small Dutch town. Eventually, Maxi and I ran out of things to do, so we spent some of Ben's downtime with him on the set. The German director, who also wrote the script, must have been homesick for German girls; he loved having Maxi and me around.

There were perhaps 100 townspeople who were cast as dead people in the film, working night and day, hoping maybe for a brief taste of

Hollywood stardom. They were all piled in a big bus wearing dead-people makeup—some green, some blue, some just white and spooky, but all looking their worst through the bus window—a strange sort of Madame Tussaud's morgue. As shocked as I was by their appearance, Maxi was really freaked out. The first time we went on the set, she nearly attacked those living corpses. Before I could catch her, she ran away from me and onto the bus barking and trying to get at them. They playfully screamed and she barked back. They screamed and she barked even more. I ran to get her, and as we escaped, the bus driver closed the door behind us. Thank God. I could see why Maxi was scared. The script was so-so, but the makeup department delivered a masterpiece.

ONE MORNING, BEN was a little careless on his way to work. At 7:00 A.M., he took Maxi outside for a potty break and some fresh morning air before returning her to me in bed for our remaining three hours of sleep. He kissed me good-bye and promised to send the driver to pick us both up for lunch. I fell back to sleep almost immediately.

Some hours later when I woke up, I realized Maxi was not in bed with me. I got up and called her. Nothing. I looked under my bed and all around the suite. I was on my knees searching behind the couches, in the bathroom, on the balcony, in the closets—everywhere—but no Maxi. I thought perhaps Ben had taken her to the set, but I knew he wouldn't have. I was beginning to panic. I don't know how long it took me to realize the main door to our suite was open a little. Now I really began to panic. I got dressed in a flash and ran to look for Maxi. She was nowhere to be found.

Alarmed, I went to the concierge and hotel manager, but they had not seen her. I even called the set to check with Ben just in case. I didn't want to scare him, so I spoke with an assistant. Maxi wasn't there either.

It was misty and foggy outside. I could hardly see my surroundings. Alone, desperate, and crying out for my little girl, I began to wander the countryside close by our hotel. The damp, lush meadows there stretched for miles. I was beginning to lose hope. I could hear sheep in every direction surrounding me. But no Maxi.

What felt like hours may have only been five minutes—but those moments of searching were some of the worst moments of my life. Maxi had disappeared.

As the fog lifted, I began to see the sheep. They were indeed everywhere wandering the green pastures all around me. Suddenly amidst all of the white clouds I noticed a tiny patch of brown. I could only hope it wasn't a mirage. Yes, out in the middle of all the sheep, there was my little brown shepherd giving orders to the herd. For a little girl, Maxi has a big, brave heart. I was thrilled to have found her but couldn't bear to interrupt her happiness. She loved playing shepherd and the sheep seemed to be having a good time too. There was certainly lots of animal talk and carrying on. When I finally did call her name, she ran to me like a speeding bullet. I thought surely one of our hearts would explode with excitement.

When we arrived back at the hotel, the manager was very relieved to see us. "Where did you find her?"

"I should have known. She was playing with the sheep. In New York, she talks with the horses in Central Park, and here in Holland, she takes care of the sheep."

"Maybe one day she will run with the elephants in Africa," he said.

"I'll bet she would enjoy it!"

Prague

*I*N 2002, WE were invited to the Czech Republic to participate in the Karlovy Vary Film Festival. We accepted happily. My mother was born in Prague, and I'd never been there. In August of 1968, Ben made a war movie titled *The Bridge at Remagen*, and he saw the Russian tanks move into that beautiful city and take away its freedom. He hadn't returned since.

Karlovy Vary had been a world-renowned health resort when the Germans occupied it and renamed the town Karlsbad. The Russians followed and let it get run down. But now it had been restored to all of its former splendor. Our hotel was a jewel with superb service.

Ben was a member of the festival's jury and was obliged to see the films in competition, which fortunately were shown in the morning. That gave us time to drive into Prague and explore the charming city. With Maxi on her leash, we walked over the Charles Bridge to the town hall and its famous moving clock. We had lunch at an outdoor

café, and strolled the narrow streets, popping into one art gallery after another. We then visited the building where Franz Kafka had lived.

On our first visit together, Ben wanted to see the International Hotel. It was from his room there that he saw the tanks enter Prague. And it was on the hotel's steps that he and several other actors waited for a car to take them out of Czechoslovakia. As we sat on those same steps, I on one side of him and Maxi on the other, it was as though she knew that something terrible had happened there.

"When the Russians were here, this city was gray, and now look at it."

"The Czechs worked a miracle, Ben. It's so beautiful."

Ben turned to me. "Listen, they're giving an outdoor performance of *Don Giovanni* tonight. Do you want to go?"

"Do you think Maxi will like it?"

"Well, whenever Mozart is playing at home, she stops what she is doing, lays her head on the floor, and listens."

"What the heck," I said, "if she gets bored, we'll take her home."

Maxi became an opera buff. The following night, she sat through an outdoor performance of *La Boheme* and listened to every aria with what I determined was pleasure.

The closing night of the festival in Karlovy Vary was an elegant affair. A lot of actors and other international celebrities were there. At our dinner table sat Harvey Keitel, Jacqueline Bisset, Elijah Wood, and fellow Cassavetes actor, Seymour Cassel. But for me the biggest excitement of the evening was meeting Václav Havel, the former president of Prague. He was seated to my left and his wife to Ben's right. He made some touching remarks, welcoming us to his country. The talk of the table was light and frothy. All heavy political subjects were avoided. We talked about film mainly, which Mr. Havel knew quite a bit about. While he and his intellectual friends were underground fighting the Russian occupiers, he, as a superb writer, was always in the company of poets, musicians, film directors, and actors.

After the dessert, we all rose to say our good-byes, when the photographers appeared and asked us to move together for a few group shots. I reached for Maxi's bag, which had been resting near my feet under the table. Her head appeared, and in that moment, I heard someone say, "Ohhh? A dachshund!"

The ex-president moved to Maxi and, with a soft hand, caressed her time and again. Something had moved him. He insisted that Maxi be near him in the photograph.

"Mr. President," I asked, "you love dogs, don't you?"

"Especially the small dachshund," he said. "I had one just like yours when I was a child. It lived to be twenty-two years old. And when he died, I cried like a baby."

"Twenty-two years is a long time, Mr. President. Please, tell me, what did you feed your dog?"

"Very good food and a lot of love," he said, continuing to caress Maxi.

Movie Star Maxi

*F*ULFILLING A PROMISE made years earlier to a film director, written and signed on a bar napkin, Ben was finally going to co-star with Rita Moreno in *Blue Moon*, a romantic film about an aging married couple. *Blue Moon* had taken some years to get off the ground. As often happens in the movie business, they were just waiting for the money. Well, they finally found it, and so they went to work. The entire movie would be shot in New York, which was fine with me.

A week before shooting began, we had a dinner party with some of the cast members including Rita Moreno and Burt Young, who played Ben's brother, along with the director John Gallagher, and the producer Ronnie Shapiro. Of course, our Maxi joined us and, like always, stayed quietly under the table in her bag. In fact, she was so quiet, she almost missed her chance to become a movie star.

During dinner, the actors and the director were discussing their characters, their scenes, and some possible script revisions. While discussing

depression and sadness, since Ben's character suffered from both, someone, I don't remember who, suggested putting a dog in the film because pets help depressive people; they are better than Prozac. The discussion went on for some time before I even thought to bring Maxi out for an audition. But my timing was perfect.

Reaching under the table and slowly lifting her onto my lap, I said, "Mr. Gallagher, I have the perfect pet for your film. Meet Madison Avenue Maxi—second generation super star!"

As soon as I said that, Maxi jumped out of my arms and ran to Ben. She let out two short barks, and Ben picked her up to receive a mouthful of kisses. It was the perfect audition.

She got the part.

In fact, they practically repeated that very same scene in the film. Maxi played Burt Young's dog. During her only scene, she ran out from a warehouse to Ben, who scooped her up into his arms as Burt's character warmly and simply suggests, "You should get a dog." And that was that. Truer words have rarely been spoken.

Maxi put in a full day on the set. She had to shoot her scene over and over so they could capture her character from every angle. When she wasn't in front of the camera, she rested comfortably in her very own director's chair, with her name on it, while Ben filmed his scenes. They worked that day from seven in the morning and didn't arrive home until after 8:00 P.M. Both of my babies were exhausted.

"How was she, Ben?"

"She made me proud. What an actress."

"Really? Was she great?"

"She was great! But no more work for my little girl. The hours are too tough. She retires with a crown. Once is enough."

"Once in a blue moon," I said with a smile.

When they finished shooting in New York, the producer announced that he wanted to take a small crew along with Ben and Rita to shoot the final scene on the streets of Paris. Their characters in the film had wished for many years to celebrate their second honeymoon in Paris, and the producer intended to make it authentic.

Ben came home singing, "I love Paris in the springtime, I love Paris in the fall, I love Paris . . ."

I knew something must be going on. My husband doesn't come home singing very often. I asked, "Ben, why do you love Paris?"

"We're going to Paris, my baby. Start the luggage."

I couldn't believe my ears. I had read the script, so I knew where the final scene took place, but where would a small, independent film get the money to spend on a long weekend for a dozen people in Paris for one scene? I said to Ben, "Are you joking?"

"Yes, this producer is a big spender. You and Maxi are invited, too."

Well, Ben wasn't joking. That producer sure was a big spender. Everything was five-star. Maxi's first trip to the city of lights was *très magnifique* and so chic. We stayed in a luxury suite at the Tremoille. We lunched at the famed restaurant Fouquets and dined at the Tour D'Argent. Maxi was in heaven. In Paris, she could sit in the open with us—even on her own chair—while she ate her gourmet carrots à la France. Bon appetit.

The shoot on the streets of Paris took only a short time after the crew set up. Ben and Rita held hands as they crossed the Champs-Élysées. Maxi and I watched with the producer as the two lovebirds took the famous Parisian boulevard by storm. They were finished in two takes. There wasn't even any dialogue to film—only Paris. That was a very expensive hour. But obviously this producer was a generous and sensitive man producing a heartwarming, romantic film. In the end, he showered everyone with lavish gifts of jewelry—blue moons in diamonds and sapphires. You don't get that even in a Hollywood production.

But all good things must come to an end. It was time to say *au revoir* to Paris. It was time for Ben to pay the piper.

Ben's Back

*B*EN'S BACK SURGERY was quick and successful. He had been complaining of lower back pain for some months, and finally, he could stand it no more and had to have the operation.

Maxi and I were waiting by his bed when he woke up. I had slipped her into his private room at the hospital. He was so happy to see our faces. The few doctors and nurses who knew she was with us politely looked the other way. Ben was feeling so good when he was discharged, after only four days in the hospital, that he insisted we walk to one of our favorite restaurants and have a plate of pasta. The surgery had made him a new man already.

When we got home, I phoned our favorite spa, and luckily, they said they would have a spacious apartment waiting for us the following week and that Maxi was also welcome, which made us happy. Of course, she couldn't join us for treatments: facials, massages, and so

forth, but it was an excellent place for Ben to have rehab for his back and for us all to recharge our batteries.

Martinis were replaced with sunshine, workouts, and healthy living. Maxi had a good time at Palm Air. We shared long walks to the fish pond and played ball on the golf course. She was really in her element there. She had great fun pushing those golf balls all over the manicured green lawns. She could play there for hours with the little white balls she found in bushes and under trees nearby. I was sure it wouldn't be long before she learned to score a hole-in-one. Certainly she improved her handicap.

Ben had a nice suntan from playing water volleyball with his twice-a-year spa buddies. It was good to see my husband back in his old element. By the time we left, we looked like two old houses with shiny new windows.

There was still about a month before his next picture started, but we were on the right track. Back in New York, our friends were full of compliments. "Oh, you look so good," they would all say. To which Ben would say with a smile, "Clean living. Clean living." Life rarely felt so good. We were back on top of the world. Feeling good really does help you look good.

And thank God for Maxi. She had been an excellent nursemaid for Ben while he was healing. With unconditional love, she bounced back and forth between us making each of us smile often and always warming our hearts.

We continued our healthy lifestyle between Madison Avenue and our home in Sag Harbor. Ben was in great shape to go to work. He had lost some pounds, and he looked healthy and wonderful. I was proud of my old man.

Maxi's First Lawn Party

THE NEWSPAPER COLUMNIST Neil Travis invited us to a late afternoon lawn party at his home in Bridgehampton. It was one of those crisp summer days; there was not a cloud in the sky. Most of the guests were dressed in summer white. Ben and I joined a group of friends with Maxi, who was resting in my arms. Somehow she got nervous. *Too many people*, I thought. After all of the hellos, hugs, and kisses, I introduced Maxi to everyone. And then there came two

 enormous dogs. Playfully they jumped on my legs to get a better look at Maxi. They almost knocked me over. Maxi let them have it with her bark, which was pretty powerful coming from such a tiny dog. I got

anxious; what should I do? Maxi was clutching and clinging more and more to my chest. And that's when I heard a voice.

"Let your dachsie down. Let her play with those boys. They won't hurt her. I had some dachshunds myself, and they were very brave. They know how to take care of themselves."

I turned around and saw it was our good friend Marty Richards. He was a dachshund expert indeed. How well I remember hearing about his beloved Hansel and Gretel. Still I was not convinced. But

when Ben arrived with our Bloody Marys, I decided to try Marty's advice and place Maxi on the ground. The big dogs made a mad dash for her, but like a torpedo, she showed them speed they never expected. Before we knew it, Maxi disappeared. Ben and I searched the grounds. It was getting dark as I walked to the beach, looking everywhere, calling Maxi; but there was no answer. I reached the water's edge, and my heart started to race when I realized Maxi would never enter that ocean.

When I returned to the house and Ben saw that Maxi was not with me, he became agitated, if not desperate. He ran inside the house looking for our girl. Just after he leaped up the wooden steps of the porch, I saw little Maxi huddled and trembling behind the stairs looking at me with her beautiful, frightened, helpless black eyes. I quickly went to pick her up. Right then Ben reappeared, looked at us curiously, and said, "Whose blood?"

I looked down and saw that my white blouse had a big red spot on it, which Maxi couldn't stop licking with her little tongue.

I noticed my empty glass and quickly realized what had happened. "No blood, Ben. Bloody Mary," I laughed.

"I'll get you another one," Ben smiled, "and one for Maxi too. You both deserve it."

The Island of Elba

$\mathcal{M}$AXI AND I were happy to join Ben in Italy again—one small, happy family. Even so, we would not be together for most of the filming. In fact, we would be staying on two separate islands. Maxi and I would stay on the island of Elba in a gorgeous hotel on the beach, while for seven weeks, six days a week, Ben stayed on the island of Pianosa in a recently closed maximum security prison not unlike Alcatraz. The conditions were modest, but the other actors and crew made the experience interesting for Ben until the mosquitoes entered the picture. They ate him alive. Each week, I covered his new bites with creams and armed him with a week's supply of combat lotion for his return to lock-up. He told me they were the size of elephants, those mosquitoes.

It was the end of the season in the Mediterranean, but it was still a beautiful September. The weather was warm. The sun was still hot during the day. Maxi would sit on the beach like my guardian angel

while I swam laps in the ocean. She watched me like a hawk, but I'm not sure what kind of lifeguard she would be if I really needed help because she doesn't like the water—especially the ocean. While we enjoyed our time on Elba, I imagine Ben was having the time of his life with his crew and the three remaining prisoners on Pianosa who were so interesting they were even included in the film.

Each week, Ben came back full of stories and tales from prison. Maxi loved every homecoming. They reunited like old lovers. We would wait down at the pier for Ben's boat to arrive. Before the boat was even attached to the dock, Maxi was in Ben's arms filling his face with her wet kisses and warm hellos.

The third week, Ben came home complaining of a terrible toothache and burning tongue.

I said immediately, "Too much peperoncino."

"Maybe. What can I do?"

"I don't know about the tongue, but I have a special powder. It should take care of your tooth." And indeed it did.

He used a lot of powder that weekend. When it came time to return to Pianosa on Sunday evening, there was no powder left. It was a stormy night, and it turned out the sea was too rough to take Ben back to prison. No boats could leave the island. For the first time, I witnessed the intensity of his pain. Ben was in agony. I tried to help him with aspirin and other painkillers, but nothing worked.

"Elke, I need a martini. Maybe that will help my toothache. This is unbearable."

I laughed and hoped he would fall asleep soon. I could tell this was serious pain. My husband is not a complainer. Monday morning, before the boat took off for prison, I went to the pharmacy to get more powder and more anti-mosquito spray.

When I saw him off, I said jokingly, "Tell your cook to take it easy on the hot pepper." And Maxi and I watched as he sailed back to prison.

Ben's toothache didn't get any better. When he phoned that night from Pianosa, he still complained of a burning sensation on his tongue and of a horrible pain in the back of his mouth. I know from personal experience that there is no ache like a toothache. My middle name is toothache. I must have visited every dentist between Brazil and Capetown. I knew if Ben was complaining, this must be a serious pain, but we still had two weeks in Italy before we could see our dentist in New York.

Luckily and strangely, the toothache disappeared as quickly and mysteriously as it came on. But the burning tongue remained.

We left Pianosa and Elba for the final week of shooting in Roma. When we arrived back at our suite at the Hotel De La Ville, I couldn't help but ask sarcastically, "Did you bring the honey, honey?"

"No honey this time, honey."

It was a spectacular and colorful October in Rome. The powder worked but Ben's tongue still burned as we made our way around the city to our favorite restaurants and piazzas. While we always enjoy the Eternal City, I was eager to get back to New York so Ben could fix his tooth and get on with his next picture in Los Angeles.

Ben had only two days in New York. Right away, he saw the dentist, but the dentist found nothing wrong. He couldn't explain the toothache or the burning tongue. So Ben was left with no alternative but to start the next film and hope for the best.

Los Angeles

*M*AXI AND I stayed in New York while Ben went off to Los Angeles for the first few weeks of shooting *Very Mean Men*.

Martin Landau, Matthew Modine, and Burt Young co-starred with Ben. Everybody loved the script. It was well written, hilarious, and touching, and they were all great in it. Unfortunately, no one ever saw the movie. After some disagreements between the producer and the filmmakers, they chose not to release it. There is no business like show business.

Well, Ben's toothache came back very strong early on during the shooting. He complained to me often by phone about the pain and the strange feeling in his tongue. It wasn't like him to complain, but I was sure he was just missing his girls. After all, the dentist had found nothing wrong.

Ben couldn't stand it any longer. His agent took him to see a specialist in Beverly Hills. He called me when he got back to his hotel with the news.

"Well, I need a biopsy. There's a benign tumor in the back of my mouth. They want to do it tomorrow."

"I am coming to LA immediately. I'll let you know when I'll be landing."

"No, it's nothing. This is kid's stuff. It's a piece of cake," Ben said.

He tried to talk me into flying the next morning, but I had already made up my mind. Maxi and I were on the plane almost before we hung up.

The news didn't get any better after we arrived in Los Angeles. Our favorite hotel for twenty years, the Sunset Marquis, wouldn't let Maxi in. Since our last stay there, it seems the entire staff had changed. On top of everything else that was happening, Ben had to pull some clout just to get us a small bungalow in the back of the property—and still we were instructed to keep Maxi in her bag at all times in the public parts of the hotel, especially in the lobby, pool area, and restaurants. It was a drag.

To make matters worse, the biopsy came back positive. Ben had cancer in his mouth.

We were devastated. There is nothing like the news of cancer. I felt like a knife had been driven through my heart, and I couldn't even imagine what Ben was feeling. I prayed that it was a small cancer. Unfortunately, it was not.

We kept the illness a secret while he bravely finished filming *Very Mean Men*. Maxi and I both wanted to be near him to comfort him as much and as often as possible. We joined him for a few days while they were shooting in the desert.

Then Maxi had her own little disaster in the desert. While making a heroic effort to climb the steel stairs into Ben's trailer, she slipped and caught her toenail in the grate. I don't know how long she must have been hanging there while I was away getting a coffee, but when I found her, she was silently crying and bleeding while her little paw hung above her head, stuck in the stairs. Almost as if she didn't want to be a burden, she didn't make a noise. Ben would have never known to come and save her. Thank God I came back when I did.

And thank God for helpful production assistants and a fast car. We sped Maxi almost an hour away to the vet who bandaged her paw up with a little white boot. My heart ached for my broken little girl.

As soon as the picture wrapped, Ben began to prepare for surgery. Except for the cancer, he was as healthy as a horse. He looked strong and virile. He was a fine example of clean living. To look at him, you would never have known the devils that were lurking in his body. Looking back, I am so glad we made those efforts to get healthy during the months before his operation.

He took full advantage of the facilities at the Sunset Marquis. He swam several times daily in the private pool off of our bungalow, and he worked out like a thirty-year-old in the gym while Maxi watched from inside her bag. Somehow he was preparing to battle for his life. He was afraid but strong—thank God we kept everything private—if anyone who knew him saw him, then they would have immediately seen the fear in his warm, powerful brown eyes and sensed the danger.

On our last day at The Sunset Marquis while we were checking out, Burt Young, who has a home next door, stopped by to say his farewells. Maxi jumped out of her bag and ran across the lobby to greet him with a mouthful of kisses.

Burt got excited and, petting her, in a high voice playfully said, "Is this my leading lady? Are you my leading lady? Is this Maxi?"

To which Maxi responded with a very warm and very wet pee-pee. She left her mark. We left the Marquis.

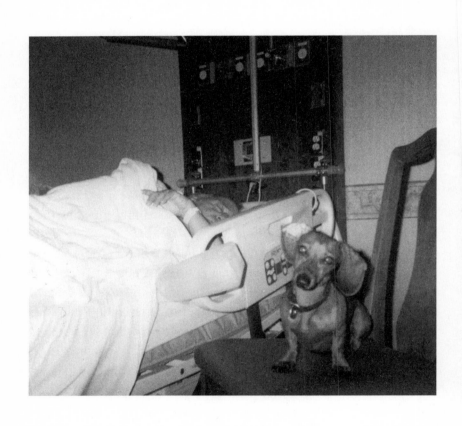

Maxi's Love

AXI AND I went with Ben to the hospital at UCLA. We checked him into a private, almost cheerful room and waited anxiously for the doctor to arrive. Ben was playing with Maxi on his bed when Dr. Berke came in.

Ben said, "Sorry, doctor. I know dogs aren't allowed."

"It's okay. I like this little guy. What is his name?"

"Her name is Maxi."

After some dog talk, the doctor excused himself. "Get some rest Ben, sleep well. I'll see you bright and early."

"You get some rest doctor because tomorrow you have to perform," Ben said.

And with that we were alone again. We had our family dinner together. Ben didn't have much of an appetite, but Maxi and I enjoyed sharing our rubber chicken.

After dinner but before bedtime, I left Maxi sleeping in Ben's arms

while I went out to charm the nurses into taking good care of my husband. They were all very nice, and I could tell immediately that Ben was in good hands. While standing at the nurse's station, I noticed the name Gazzara written first on the schedule board along with a bunch of other patients' names and the times of their procedures next to their names. Apparently Ben's operation was scheduled from 7:30 until 11:00.

When I got back to the room, both of my babies were sound asleep. I sat with them quietly for some time. I looked at Ben sleeping there and was flooded with memories of our years together. What an interesting life. We had traveled the world, had millions of ups and downs, made some good friends, and were finally able to appreciate life's healthy moments together. And now, for the first time, I wondered how many more years we had left. I wanted so badly to climb into bed with them both and wake up after a good night's sleep to find out we were only having a bad dream. No such luck.

I must have dozed off a little too because Maxi startled me with a bark when the door opened. The nurses came by to take care of Ben for the night, and it was almost time for me to say good-night as well. After they left, I hugged my husband for a long time with Maxi between us like a little baby.

"By the way Ben, you got top billing tomorrow. You're the first one on the set at seven-thirty A.M. And it looks like you're through before lunch—around eleven or so."

He looked at me with his strong brown eyes and said, "Kid's stuff."

I left the hospital hoping to God that he was right.

I HAD FOUND a cozy hotel in nearby West Hollywood where I would stay with Maxi. My friend Chrissie came in from Laguna to stay with us. It was a short night. We didn't sleep much. My alarm went off at 6:00 A.M. and I was at the hospital before 7:00 A.M. I wanted to comfort Ben and give him a big smile before he went into his operation.

But his room was empty already when I arrived. They had started early. I knew I had a few hours before the operation was over, so I went for breakfast with Chrissie and Maxi. I was very nervous and couldn't eat much. My thoughts were all with Ben. Maxi's appetite was left unchanged. She ate enough for both of us.

We arrived back to the hospital in plenty of time—well before 11:00 A.M. I left Chrissie and Maxi on a bench outside with their toys and books and things spread out all around them while I went in to check on Ben. I was surprised when he still wasn't out by noon. Little did I know; he wouldn't even be out before midnight.

The hours crawled by. No one had any news for me. Now and then I would join Chrissie and Maxi for a taste of sunshine outside, but mostly, I sat glued to my chair waiting for Ben to come out. Around 7:00 P.M., Dr. Berke finally emerged.

I jumped out of my seat and ran to him, "Is everything okay doctor? How did it go?"

"I think we got it all out. He's gonna be fine."

"Can I see him."

"Not yet. It's going to be a while. My part is finished, but the plastic surgeon just started."

"So long, doctor? What happened? I thought he would be finished at eleven this morning."

The doctor gave me a patient smile and, holding my arm gently, said, "No Mrs. Gazzara, that was eleven P.M. Ben's cancer was very bad and it will take nearly as long to rebuild his face as it took to remove the tumors."

I took a moment to digest his words. How bad was "very bad"? What did he mean by "rebuild his face"? Poor Ben, I thought to myself.

"I had no idea, Doctor. Thank you for your hard work," I said.

I couldn't help but worry. Still, I was happy that Ben went to sleep expecting a simple three-hour procedure. It was an honest but good mistake.

The next seven hours passed almost as slowly as the first. I must admit I was shocked to hear how severe Ben's case really was, but I was glad to at least have some news. Chrissie and I memorized the wallpaper in the cafeteria while Maxi slept almost the whole evening in her bag. I was shivering from the cool night air and from my nerves. It wasn't until perhaps 2:00 A.M. or 2:30 A.M. that the operation was finally finished.

When I first saw Ben, I couldn't believe my eyes. He looked like a monster. His famous face was completely unrecognizable and swollen to almost four times its size. There were also bandages covering his arm and leg where they had removed skin to graft into his mouth. There were tubes coming out of everywhere. Besides the initial shock of seeing him in this state, I was most shocked to see that they had given him a tracheotomy. The nurses wheeled him straight from the operating room into the intensive care unit. I was sure Maxi would not like to see her father like this.

BEN REMAINED IN intensive care for the next three weeks. So for three weeks, we made the bench in front of the hospital our little headquarters. Maxi and Chrissie played outside on the grass with balls and toys. Thank goodness for the great LA weather. Sometimes Chrissie read while Maxi slept in the sunshine. I bounced back and forth between them and Ben's bedside. He was looking better every day but still had a long way to go before a full recovery.

He asked constantly for Maxi, so my brain was always looking for a way to sneak her into the intensive care unit. Unlike the rest of the hospital, animals were strictly forbidden in ICU. But it wasn't long before the answer walked right in front of my eyes.

A young Japanese lady entered the hospital with a medium-sized dog on a leash and walked past security—no questions asked. Well, except for me, I asked.

I found out there is a program for dogs to visit terminally ill patients in the hospital. It is called PAC, which stands for People-Animal Connection. The dogs are specially trained to give love and affection. Each PAC dog wears a red bandanna that serves as its hospital passport.

Well, I don't know any dog with more love and affection than Maxi, and even though Ben was thankfully not terminal, that night I put my plan into action and Maxi had her own red bandanna the very next day.

During the changing of the guard, I took a deep breath and walked confidently toward the security checkpoint. Maxi was in her bag with her head sticking out wearing her new red bandanna. My heart was in my throat, so I'm glad the guard spoke first.

"PAC?" he asked.

I simply smiled, nodded, and walked toward the elevator still holding my breath. I wanted to run, but I didn't dare. Step one accomplished; now if I could just get Maxi into intensive care and keep her quiet when she first sees our Frankenstein.

With wobbly legs, I approached the intensive care unit. Luckily all of the nurses I saw were huddled in the corner talking and laughing.

Nobody even paid attention to our entrance. I held my breath again and opened the door to the room. We slipped inside quietly and closed the door behind us.

Ben's bed was the first in line of eight all separated by long white curtains. There was a nurse at the far end attending to one of the patients, but most of the other curtains were closed. The intensive care unit was loud as always but not loud enough to hide a bark should Maxi decide to join in the commotion. I knew we didn't have much time. Once inside Ben's curtain, I was surprised to find him asleep. I sat down quickly with Maxi's bag on my lap and brought her head out.

It had been almost two weeks and Ben looked much better, but he was still far from his old self. I gently took his frail hand and carefully placed it on Maxi's little face and, with a soft whimpering sound, she sniffed and licked her daddy's hand until he woke up. What a moment! Ben's eyes lit up and he smiled the best crooked smile I had seen in those two weeks. Maxi's little tail was wagging happily. She was so excited to be with Ben again. I was proud of myself; I knew that there was no prescription drug that could have helped him make a quicker recovery. I didn't want Ben to see me crying, so I choked back my tears.

When it was time to leave, Maxi and I escaped the same way we came in—right through the front door. She had behaved like an angel and brought plenty of love and affection to her daddy. But I never tried that trick again. It was too much for my nerves.

During Ben's final week in the hospital, Maxi and I celebrated Thanksgiving alone on our bench in the park at UCLA with a California roll from the hospital cafeteria that was so hard it sat like a stone in my stomach. Maxi ate more than her share and didn't seem to mind the old rice. We had been invited to Laguna to share the holiday with Chrissie and her sister Doris. Ben even insisted that I go, but I couldn't leave him alone. So, while he was fed from his tubes, Maxi and I sat alone with our sushi. Nothing traditional that year.

Because we were keeping Ben's illness private at that time, I had not phoned any friends of ours in Los Angeles. Looking back, I don't think it was right. We didn't want to burden anyone, and Ben was even concerned that it could hurt his career if the news got out. So, after weeks of ordering takeout from Kentucky Fried Chicken, Taco Bell, or Mongolian Soup Bowl in order to avoid going to restaurants where I might see familiar faces and be left to explain, Maxi and I had to make the best of our Thanksgiving alone. Still, not seeing any friendly faces or talking with people I love about all that was happening was beginning to take its toll on me. How often I cried myself to sleep.

During these endless weeks while Ben was hospitalized, I really began to understand why dogs are called "man's best friend." Maxi was surely a girl's best friend. She kept me from falling into a dark hole. Whether resting peacefully beside my leg, playing joyfully with her ball, or simply sitting with me in the park on our bench—that dog saved my life while the doctors were saving Ben's.

When it came time for Ben to check out of the hospital, the doctors wanted him to remain in the Los Angeles area for another few weeks so that they could keep an eye on him and check on his progress. They also suggested that he stay until after the New Year to start his six weeks of radiation therapy. We compromised and stayed only for the three weeks. Ben wanted to be in New York for radiation.

We spent those three weeks in Laguna. Chrissie and her sister, Doris, were excited to welcome us all into their home. Ben wanted a hotel, but I needed friends around, and these friends I have known for thirty years; they are like family. Thankfully, Ben agreed.

We all giggled our days away and spent the evenings watching movies and eating great food. Those girls love to eat. Ben was eating only small bites here and there—I don't know how he survived on those little portions, but I was happy to see him eating at all. We all pampered him while he was healing. He had his own room where he could watch his sports and sleep as much as he wanted. In this house of women, he was the king of the harem. There was a nurse who came often to change his bandages and a masseuse who came not often enough to massage us all. Maxi was his favorite concubine; she was so thrilled to have her daddy back that she hardly left his side. My best friend was cheating on me with her new best friend, my very own husband. But I was comfortable with the sacrifice because I was sure she was helping him heal. We enjoyed long walks by the ocean. Laguna Beach was the perfect place at the perfect time.

Those weeks in Laguna were a delight in spite of the circumstances. Ben's checkups all went well—the cancer was gone as far as they could tell. But we had been warned that the worst was yet to come. Leaving Laguna wasn't easy. The girls had made us feel at home. And while New York is always magical during the Christmas season, there wasn't much to look forward to with these radiation treatments right around the corner.

I can't imagine that Maxi could be happy to leave Laguna either. Besides the food that she could steal from Chrissie and Doris behind my back, she enjoyed so much the sunshine that filled their house and the open space in the yard where she could run for days and chase birds, balls, and bugs. New York, on the other hand, was cold, and she would have to play indoors. Still, she was a good sport.

By the time we left Laguna, Ben's face was returning to normal. The swelling was almost gone, the stitches were long gone, he had grown a beard to cover the scars, and his spirits were lifted. Ben was a changed man already. The poison was gone from his body. Even though it was a hard ride, I was happy to have my husband back.

BY NOW, A true frequent flier, Maxi joined us on the red-eye back to New York just in time to celebrate Christmas. Danja surprised us with a colorful, happy Christmas tree in our apartment. It was nice to come home and find that Christmas had arrived early. We spent the season with family and close friends whom we had broken the news to, but we hardly spoke of the illness. Maxi braved the cold again and even seemed to enjoy the city's snowfalls and chilly temperatures.

That year I bought Maxi her first designer dog coat. It wasn't easy finding a coat that fit her long body. Every coat she tried on left her tail end hanging in the wind. Eventually we found an off-white, wool coat that did fit, but she looked like a pig in a blanket wearing it. I hated the coat, Ben hated it, but it kept her warm.

Christmas came and went too quickly. Radiation was waiting for Ben in the New Year. What a way to begin the new millennium. Maxi, Ben, and I celebrated quietly with our close friends the Koneckys and their poodle Kate. It was not quite the bubbling I had hoped for in my champagne glass to ring in a new century, but it was actually sweeter than champagne and exactly what we needed.

Radiation started off easy. Ben, Maxi, and I all went down to Beth Israel Hospital every day. Maxi got to know the way very well. Often the snows were high and always the days were freezing. It was a bitter January. It didn't take long for what was easy to become very hard,

almost impossible to endure. Ben's mouth began to blister. His throat closed tighter and tighter. He lost even more weight, and his energy was running very low. After only three weeks of daily treatments, he became a zombie. He was no longer able to eat solid food, relying instead on Ensure and other liquid nutrition for meals. Even those wouldn't sustain him though. I began to worry. Ben was very weak. He had lost too much weight.

One day after treatment, we were home and I was preparing to go out for some chores. Ben was in the kitchen trying hard to choke down one of his nutrition drinks.

"I'm taking Maxi with me, Ben. She must want some fresh air."

"Leave her here. It's too cold. She's been out already."

"Are you sure? Don't you want to lie down? I may be gone for a while."

"Go my baby. Have a good time. Maxi and I will be fine."

Well, I didn't get very far. The front door hadn't even closed behind me before Maxi came running out after me barking and barking. She was obviously trying to tell me something very important. I knew immediately that something was wrong.

I rushed back inside and followed Maxi's lead to the kitchen. Ben was lying on the floor motionless. His nutrition drink had splashed all over the floor and cabinets.

He attempted to reach for me saying only, "Help me up."

I took him in my arms and right away phoned 911.

Maxi took advantage of the commotion and cleaned up the entire mess with her eager and very fast little tongue. At least somebody enjoyed that awful drink.

I said to Ben, "That's it. We are putting you in a hospital where they will feed you through a tube. It should have been done from the beginning."

And so our little family piled into the ambulance, and with a loud siren pushing us through the snowy New York traffic, we arrived pretty quickly downtown at Beth Israel Hospital where they did just that.

The doctors inserted the feeding tube and started Ben on a heavy dose of morphine to ease his pain. I was waiting alone in his room when they brought him back from the operation. I watched as the nurses and doctors wheeled a lot of machinery in with him. He was hooked up to a heart monitor, breathing support, and several IVs. There were bags of blood, food, and medicine. My husband was really a mess again. For the first time, I was actually petrified that I might lose Ben.

Once everything was settled I spoke with the nurses about getting a mattress next to Ben's bed. The best they could offer was a very thin mat that I could unroll on the floor along with a polyester blanket that was full of holes—but I would have settled for anything just to be near to my favorite patient.

I knew that I needed to stay with Ben around the clock. He was very weak, undernourished, dehydrated, and was only halfway through his six-week radiation hell. He would need to be hospitalized for at least the remaining three weeks of treatment. I wanted to stay by his side the whole time. Unfortunately, even though Maxi had just saved Ben's life, she wasn't allowed to stay with us in the hospital, and I hadn't had time yet to see if her red bandanna would work here.

Danja had been suffering from some emotional turmoil, so she wasn't capable of taking Maxi while I stayed with Ben. I phoned a couple of friends and worked out a schedule for them to keep Maxi. Thank God for our dear friend Douglas Ladnier who was engaged at night performing on Broadway in *Jekyll & Hyde*. He was at the hospital in a flash to take Maxi. She loved Douglas. I knew that she would be in good hands.

I HARDLY SLEPT the first night while Ben never opened his eyes. I thought of Maxi and how much I wished she were sleeping next me. I'm sure I would have found sleep with her.

The next morning, I phoned Douglas first thing to see how things were going. What a relief. Douglas calmed me down with his beautiful baritone voice. "Don't worry. She's fine. How's Ben?"

"Ben is sleeping. Tell me something cheerful. Tell me about Maxi."

"Well, she made her Broadway debut last night."

"Did she get all of her words right?"

"She was a diva and then she slept the whole night you know where."

"Under the covers between your legs, right?"

"You got it. The best lover I've had in weeks," Douglas laughed.

"I wish I could say the same. You should see my funny bed here. And what about Baby? Was your cat jealous?"

"They got along like sisters. Maxi wanted to play, Baby batted her away, and then they both joined me in bed for the night. They were precious."

"What a happy trio. Thank you Douglas for your great help. Come by later. I'd love to give Maxi some kisses and take you to lunch."

I relaxed knowing that Maxi was happy and enjoying her time with Douglas and Baby. I turned my attention back to Ben. In those first days, I learned to sterilize and clean his tubes and replace his food bags. Meanwhile, Ben was completely out of it. Even when he was awake, he hallucinated that his room was filled with Fellini and a cast of deceased Italian actors. It was quite a circus, literally. One time the morphine even helped him conjure flying monkeys. It was alternatively either funny or very scary. I wasn't sure how to react.

Douglas kept Maxi for two weeks. During that time, I was only able to smuggle her in to see Ben twice at night when the lovely night nurse, my new very best friend, politely closed his eyes and let us in. I had made my plans very carefully. Each time, I picked her up from Douglas downstairs in her bag in front of the main entrance of the hospital after his show. It was late and dark, and no other visitors were coming in and out. I held Maxi's bag like an overnight purse on my shoulder, and the guard didn't even know she was there. He must have thought I was bringing fresh clothes for myself. No questions were asked. When we got up to Ben's floor, I showed Maxi to my friend the nurse and asked him to help Ben get to the bathroom so I could surprise him with his baby. All went well. The nurse played his part brilliantly, and when Ben was safely in the bathroom with his various IVs and tubes in place, I sneaked Maxi in through the crack in the bathroom door and closed it very fast behind her. I heard through the door Ben and Maxi exchanging wet kisses and warm hellos. Her familiar "I love you, I love you, I love you" bounced off the sterile walls and warmed my heart. I prayed no one heard her through the closed door.

Each time he saw her, I saw him getting better in front of my very eyes. It was amazing and actually unbelievable. Maxi was a miracle worker. She couldn't come often, but when she did, it really made a difference.

Ben was gaining weight and getting stronger. The radiation was still torture, but the end was in sight. Life at the hospital became monotonous and boring. I was an expert nurse by then, able to take care of Ben's hourly needs. I could easily change his food and keep him comfortable. I took my new profession so seriously that I changed rubber gloves more often than the busiest nurse.

DURING THE FINAL week, Maxi had an exciting trip to take with our friend Nancy Merill to her home in Rheinbeck with her two bichon frise, which are slightly smaller but twice as furry as Maxi. Actually they look like little powder puffs.

It was hard enough having her stay in the city with Douglas, but it was impossible having her stay with Nancy so far away. Ben became crazy. After only five days, he began demanding, "Where is Maxi? Phone Nancy. I want Maxi back here today. I want my dog."

"Ben, Maxi is fine, but I will talk to Nancy tonight and see if she can bring her in tomorrow."

I had been with Ben so long in the hospital I hadn't even noticed that we were in the middle of a New York blizzard. We would be lucky to see Maxi in a week much less a day. They were snowed in—or snowed out, as the case may be. As crazy as Ben got, there was no fighting Mother Nature; we couldn't get Maxi back until the weather cleared.

THE NEXT DAY, I entered Ben's room with a smile. "Happy Valentine's Day *mein geliebt*," I said as I kissed his forehead and handed him a large bouquet of red roses.

"Thank you my angel. The doctors wouldn't let me out to go to Tiffany. We'll celebrate when I'm out of here. I love you."

BEN DRIFTED OFF but awoke almost immediately calling for Maxi. "Elke, put her on my bed now," he said.

"Maxi is not here, Ben. She is still snowed in."

"Your friend is stealing our dog," Ben growled and, growing even more excited, said, "Put her on the phone. If she doesn't bring me my dog, I'll send someone to get her."

"Ben, stop it. You are paranoid; who are you going to send? Go back to sleep, my baby. Maxi will be home soon."

Just then, with the most perfect timing, there was a soft knock on the door. The doctors rarely knock, and we weren't expecting any visitors, but sometimes surprise guests are the best guests of all.

Nancy must not have even known how difficult it was to bring a dog into the hospital. Ignorance is bliss. She arrived unexpected but right on time with our little Maxi. The mood in the room changed so suddenly and so completely that it was as if the sun rose after days of darkness. We only had two days left in the hospital, so I didn't even care that Maxi was loud with her love. She soon settled in comfortably next to Ben on his bed. His eyes filled with tears. It was a very emotional reunion. Maxi spent much of that day with us in the hospital room. Very soon, we would all sleep together at home again.

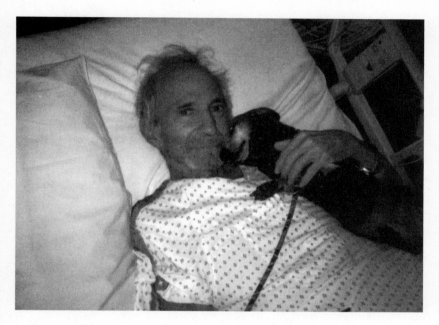

During the last two days at the hospital, I was back on full-time nurse duty. I wanted to make sure I was fully prepared to take care of Ben once we went home. When we left the hospital, they gave me enough rubber gloves to take care of a small army. For the next fourteen months, I would play the part of Florence Nightingale to my soldier. And Maxi would be my partner in healing.

Ben still looked very thin and fragile when we finally left the hospital after three weeks of intense treatments. Maxi stayed glued to his lap. She was so happy to have her family back together again.

Ben didn't need my gourmet cooking, but he did need me to prepare his liquid meals five times a day. And there was the daily regimen of cleaning tubes and bags and nursing his wounds. Maxi cleaned up after me in the kitchen whenever she could and stayed by her daddy's side always. When she wasn't sound asleep on his lap, she was pushing one of her balls around his feet so that he would play with her. She kept his spirits up and I overheard many sweet conversations between them. Maxi was a blessing.

The next three months were a blur of doctors' appointments, trips back and forth to Sag Harbor, and minor daily improvements. During the spring months, Danja and I would steal Maxi from Ben's arms while he was sleeping to take her for afternoon walks in the park. It was good for us girls to get some fresh air, and I enjoyed bonding with my daughter again. Maxi also seemed to really enjoy having both of her mommies around to play with.

I stuffed Ben with my own version of designer nutrition drinks. Even though he couldn't taste what I prepared for him because he was eating through a tube inserted straight into his stomach, I still used a lot of love and the freshest fruits when preparing his bag. He was a happy and thankful customer. "It needs more garlic," he even once joked.

Ben and I decided to get away one weekend, so we took Maxi with us to Sag Harbor. Ben was getting stronger every day—the feeding tube was working full time. He still couldn't eat, but he often enjoyed watching me wine and dine. Even when he's healthy, Ben doesn't eat fish, so I took the opportunity on a sunny Sunday afternoon to go to lunch at one of my favorite seafood restaurants in Montauk. As always, Maxi joined us in her bag and was behaving like a little princess.

We were seated at a big, private booth near the center of the restaurant with tall dividers. I ordered the largest, well-fed lobster on the menu. When it arrived, I could tell Ben was going to be very happy watching me devour this enormous animal that was the same red as our fake-leather booth. Maxi also doesn't care for fish, so she slept quietly in her bag next to Ben leaving me, for once, to eat in peace. I was in heaven.

I must have been so caught up in that crustacean that I hadn't noticed the family sitting in the booth behind Ben. Suddenly Maxi jumped out of her bag and gave us quite a scare. I looked up and saw the head of a small infant sticking up over the booth. In that instant, Maxi snatched something from the baby's mouth. The baby was in shock and didn't move. I was frozen. Maxi was back in her bag almost as quickly as she had jumped out only now with her new toy. Our little princess had taken the pacifier straight from the baby's mouth! Thank God the parents had not seen the exchange at all. Ben got up quickly to check on the situation. The boy was completely unharmed. Maxi had only taken what she wanted—a precision strike—mission accomplished. It took some time before I could breathe again. I'm so glad that baby wasn't hurt. I still get goose bumps when I think about it. What a wake-up call. Now we know we have a first-class thief in our family. I think Maxi would steal the glasses from a blind man.

EVENTUALLY, BEN WAS healthy enough to work again. His next picture would shoot in Italy. He was afraid it was coming too soon. His voice was still shaky, and he was in speech therapy every day to prepare. As the time came closer for us to leave, Ben was full of doubt. He didn't think he was ready to work again, but a man like Ben needs to work—not just for the money but for the work itself, for the art. Also, it makes my and Maxi's lives easier when he is busy. So we were all happy to have him back in action.

The director, who had worked with Ben before, flew in from Rome to meet with him and provide encouragement. It turned out that what they were most interested in was having Ben act in the picture—the voice would be overdubbed in Italian by Giancarlo Giannini, so there was nothing to be concerned about.

Within a few weeks, we flew with Maxi to Italy. Our luggage was particularly full for this trip—we were like a flying pharmacy. I had packed enough cans of every flavor of Ensure to keep Ben alive for years even though we were only going for some months. The picture would shoot in Turin and wrap in Barcelona.

The hotel in Turin didn't want a dog, but they did want Ben, so we were allowed to stay there with Maxi. Apparently, though, Maxi wasn't the only dog allowed. The owner's German shepherd was also a frequent guest. One morning after Ben had left for shooting, Maxi and I had just finished breakfast and were in the lobby talking with the owner. During our conversation about good local restaurants, we were ambushed by his big beast. The shepherd ran out from the owner's office and grabbed Maxi by the neck and began swinging her back and forth like a dead rabbit. Luckily, Maxi was already on her leash ready for her walk. I screamed and grabbed the leash down closer to her body and began swinging it like a lasso over my head trying to remove her from the bigger dog's mouth. The shepherd was only playing, so he let go easily when the owner got a hold of him. Unfortunately, Maxi was scared shitless, literally. While she was in the air, she lost control of her bowels and the stuff squirted all over the lobby, all over my clothes, all over the owner, and even all over the shepherd. It was an absolute mess. She had left her mark again in 3another hotel lobby—generous to a fault.

EVERY DAY DURING the filming, Maxi and I joined Ben on the set three or more times for a private feeding. No one, including the director, knew that Ben had recently battled cancer successfully, and no one knew what we were doing all of those times in his trailer. They must have thought we were still young lovers on our honeymoon enjoying the throws of passion. In reality, each time, I was filling his bag with the nutritious ingredients and medicines and plugging it into the tube discreetly coming out of his stomach. It took about a half an hour for the food to go from the bag into his body. Maxi would often sit by his side or on his lap while he "ate."

Our daily activity went unnoticed in Turin. It wasn't until the film was about to wrap in Barcelona that the secret got out. One day after I had plugged Ben in, Maxi was resting comfortably on his lap with a carrot, when there came an unexpected knock on the trailer door. It was Ben's director. I tried to quickly cover the hanging bag of food and remain discreet, but it was too late. He had already stuck his head inside the door and obviously become aware of our little charade. Maxi barked, like she would for any intruder, but that didn't help either. He saw and he knew. He was very gracious and even encouraging; assuring Ben he had a long life of work ahead of him in spite of his illness. I think he knew all along.

BEN FINISHED HIS work in the film, and we went straight to Umbria for some rest and relaxation. I wrapped his midsection with cellophane to keep his wound dry so he could swim laps in our Olympic-sized pool. The exercise and the sunshine were making my husband strong again. Maxi played with him by the pool, pushing her ball in the water and barking relentlessly waiting for him to return it. I joined

them occasionally for some fun in the sun, and we played the days away waiting for our houseguests from Spain and America to arrive.

I spent the summer making sweet milkshakes full of delicious fruits and Ben's medications. Maxi's favorite was a banana shake. She waited eagerly for drops to fall to the floor, and once or twice, she even grabbed the empty rubber food bag from the trash can. She tore it open and licked it clean. When she was done, there wasn't a drop of food left in the bag. I was concerned the first time when I remembered there was lithium in it, but I watched her closely and she was as playful as ever that day. Maybe even a little happier than usual; I noticed that we suddenly had a little drummer in the house. Her tail was knocking on everything as she bounced from room to room.

We had some important birthdays that summer. Ben turned seventy and Maxi three. Douglas came over from New York to celebrate his thirtieth. For his party, we invited our friend, the great Spanish painter, Jorge Castillo and his lovely bride Yola. Gabrielle, a fine Italian sculptor, also came in from Rome with two delicious home-made cakes from his talented sister. Our housekeepers Franca and Bruno cooked up a storm.

The evening ended with a double surprise. After some bottles of wine, we discovered it was also Jorge's birthday—even more reason to continue our celebration. Anna Maria and Michele invited us to their medieval tower in the sixteenth-century village of Toscolano. There was a light mist in the air that made the tower even more alluring. We saw something special happening in the sky and wanted a better view. Jorge carried Maxi in his arms up the spiral staircase leading to the second floor. We all followed close behind, and sure enough, looking out the tiny tower windows, we saw the most beautiful sight. In the twilight hours, with the sun falling just below the horizon, there were not one but two gigantic rainbows illuminating the sky with every imaginable color. None of us had ever seen that before. It was spectacular. Maxi began to howl. She was talking to the rainbows as if they were a full moon.

For her party, Maxi had several friends over. They each had their own bowls with grilled chicken, some carrots, and, of course, birthday cookies. After lunch, Maxi led the pack down to her favorite meadow where our grapes are eaten by the wild boars. We hear them often at

night but have never seen them during the day. What damage they have done. Those pigs have no mercy. As angry as they make Ben, he was now just as happy to watch Maxi play with her friends in that same field.

The summer wrapped up with a nice visit from Danja and Chrissie and Doris. Ben started to eat solid foods again, a little pasta very wet with sauce, and was even beginning to enjoy a watered-down glass of wine some nights. We attended festivals from Todi to Spoleto. Out under the stars, Maxi saw and heard the most amazing *Rigoletto* and the finest flamenco performances. At one performance in Todi, at the end of the flamenco dance when the audience burst into applause, Maxi joined them and filled the whole piazza with her echoing barks. The dancers took their bows and even included Maxi in their thank-you speech.

"*Gracie, gracie a tutti. Gracie* bow-wow," the lead dancer said with a laugh. And the whole audience laughed too. It was a great way to end the evening and our summer. Maxi became the star of the festival.

We were more than halfway through the year 2000 and it was time to head back to Madison Avenue. Maxi was about to make her big-screen debut. *Blue Moon* was premiering in New York. Once again the producer spared no expense. He threw a lavish dinner party and gave a generous after-party too, all as a benefit for orphans. Maxi was a movie star in the picture! When she came on the screen, I was so proud that I poked Ben perhaps a bit too hard with my elbow, forgetting his tube. But I was just so ecstatic. She was great! In the final, she was credited as "Dog—Maxi Gazzara." We were beaming-proud parents. I think Ben enjoyed watching her more than he did himself. I thought they were both outstanding.

Ben was patiently taking daily speech lessons, but no matter how hard he tried to improve, his mouth remained a problem. To encourage him to go, Maxi often joined him. They went off through the park together to meet his teacher. Ben was working very hard to rehabilitate and Maxi was there to help. The lessons were successful and Ben improved so quickly that some days I half expected Maxi to come home speaking some new words too. Wishful thinking. How often I had hoped that she could speak—perhaps it's better, though, just to read her intelligent eyes.

Thank goodness for Maxi. She gave Ben comfort and company. He practiced his lessons with her at his side every day nonstop. Later she was at his side constantly as he began serious work on his memoirs.

Charities and theater events kept us busy for the winter months. We also went to noontime movies where Maxi waited anxiously for her few bites of popcorn before nodding off. I cooked at home a lot to be sure the food was right for Ben's palate. The blender was my best friend in the kitchen. Everything had to be small for Ben to swallow. My very best friend in the kitchen, though, was Maxi. She was standing next to me watching my every move like a ping-pong game—from the counter to my hand, from my hand to the sink—her eyes never left the food. Sometimes I wonder if it's me she loves or the food! Maxi likes fruits and vegetables, nuts, yogurt, cottage cheese, melons, sweet apples, pears, string beans, asparagus, carrots, and, of course, potatoes. *Kartoffen*—that's the German side of her.

Argentina

*W*E ARRIVED IN Argentina to great fanfare. We had been invited to Mara del Plata where they were doing a retrospective of Ben's work. We flew first to Buenos Aires and immediately caught a connecting flight to Mara del Plata. The customs officials awarded Maxi a "guide dog" sticker that allowed her to accompany us everywhere. She was not only able to join us for movies, but also every night at the best *churrascaria* where they are famous for their fine meats. Maxi was in South American heaven. Our hotel was brand new and absolutely beautiful. We had a big suite and Maxi was their first four-legged customer.

The film festival began that very evening. On our way to the theater, Maxi joined us for an unexpected cocktail. We had just finished ours and were saying good-bye to some friends in the bar when one of them spilled his entire beer on the floor. The mop came too late—Maxi had cleaned the marble floor in a few split seconds. Now she would be not only jet-lagged, but also a little drunk for the first screening.

Maxi spent most of the movie snoring not so quietly on her back in her bag between Ben and me. When we walked out of the theater, there were people everywhere—camera crews, photographers, and fans. They escorted Ben to a square right in front of the entrance where the fresh cement was waiting for his handprints.

As soon as she saw Ben bending down, not to be left out, Maxi broke free from me and ran to Ben's side. He seized the opportunity. All of the people began to cheer, and Maxi politely offered her paws as Ben carefully placed them in the wet cement under his own new handprints. Another first! It wasn't quite the Hollywood walk of fame, but it was still a great place to leave their marks!

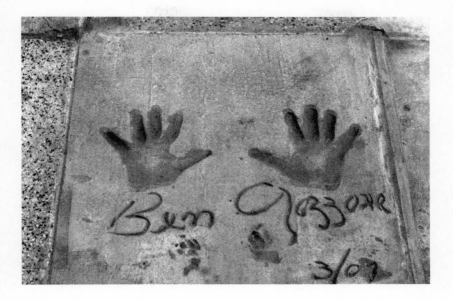

BACK IN NEW YORK, Ben was filming his Emmy Award-winning performance in *Hysterical Blindness* with our very close friend Gena Rowlands. Then something odd happened. Maxi began losing her fur. She was acting normal and didn't otherwise seem sick at first. Our vet didn't know what it was. He tried injections, creams, and even special shampoo, but nothing worked. As time went by, I began to notice Maxi was even starting to feel sick. Her fur was really falling out now, leaving small bald spots on her body.

Thank God she couldn't see herself, but even so, I bought her a little doggie T-shirt to cover her back and protect her raw skin from the sun. I bathed her lovingly every day. I got the name of a new vet from one of Ben's costars, Uma Thurman. She too was confused about Maxi's condition.

One day, I put Maxi in her T-shirt, and we went downtown to a huge dachshund gathering in Union Square Park. There were hundreds of little sausage dogs—some were dressed in the most outrageous costumes—there were dogs in tutus and tiroler hats, some wore feather boas, and some wore boots. Maxi didn't look so out of place at all in her little too-short T-shirt. She drew the most attention though from her leash that I brought over from Italy—a chain with plastic sausages for links. It looked almost real.

It was one of the other dachshund owners at the gathering who explained to me what was happening with Maxi's fur. Squirrel droppings, that was the problem. Central Park squirrel droppings.

The solution was simple: no more rolling around in the park and a lot more baths with a special medicated dog shampoo. It didn't take long for Maxi's fur to come back better than ever. I'm sure her weekly egg is also a big benefit. I wish it would work for my hair, too.

Marco Island

SIX MONTHS OR so after his surgery, Ben was still recovering. He was half his normal size. We'd received yet another lovely invitation, this time to a film festival on Marco Island in Florida. It was arranged by some even lovelier people, including the mother of Tom Cruise, an adorable lady.

When we arrived in Miami, we were picked up by a big white limousine that would take us to Marco Island. The driver warned us that Maxi should go potty before we left because there would be no stopping in alligator alley—a dangerous portion of the highway between the city and the island.

"What is alligator alley?" I asked.

"You will see."

I trusted him and went for a stroll with Maxi near the airport before we took off. And I'm glad I did. Not long after leaving Miami, the stretch of road was surrounded by swamps. Maxi sat on Ben's lap and stared

protectively out the window. I couldn't believe my eyes. What I thought were many logs turned out to be more alligators than I could even count.

The next few minutes turned out to be better than a script writer could have imagined. The driver was forced to brake quickly when one of two sparring alligators suddenly appeared on the road in front of us. Luckily, it was daylight, and the driver was quick to swerve the car to avoid running over them.

"You almost had a handbag," Ben said.

"He looks like a suitcase to me."

I still don't know if it was a coincidence or if the driver was playing a trick on us or if it was real, but at that very moment, the car stalled. In front of us was a large alligator lying in the street. Beside me to my left sat my husband, helpless with Maxi on his lap and to my right was the legendary Celeste Holmes who was also being honored at the festival. Just outside of our window was a swamp with alligators everywhere. We all began to panic.

Maxi made strange barking noises and the rest of us nervously chatted while the driver phoned for a replacement car. It wasn't long before another white stretch appeared to take us away from the jungle. The alligator had long left the road, but there were still too many to count. I scooped Maxi into my arms and quickly jumped from one car to the other. Ben was brave. He walked with bravado like Crocodile Dundee to the new car. The driver was kind enough to walk with Celeste, and soon enough, we were all safe and on our way to the island again.

Our arrival was worth the scary trip. Marco Island is gorgeous. There, Maxi brought us another great break. Because of her, we were not allowed to stay at the hotel where the rest of the festival partici-pants were staying—instead, we had one of the most elegant villas existing on the island with a pool surrounded by breathtaking outdoor decks and terraces.

We didn't have much time before we had to be at the opening ceremony. In fact, we were already delayed. While I was preparing our outfits for opening night, Ben and Maxi were investigating the unbelievable house. After some unpacking, I came out of the enormous walk-in closet with a blue suit in my right hand and gray suit in my left for Ben's approval. I saw him standing with Maxi just across the room, admiring our new surroundings. As I approached them, I heard—then felt—a big, dull bang. It took me some moments to realize that I had hit a glass door and that I was falling backward like a bowling pin. Ben and Maxi must have run like the wind because the suits had barely hit the ground before they were at my side. I saw so many stars; I thought my eyes would pop out of my head. Maxi was soon on my stomach licking my face. She couldn't stop kissing me, and while Ben ran for ice cubes, I swelled up like a balloon.

I tried to ice my face before we left the house, but we were distracted again, this time by Maxi. While we were tending to my wounds, she was enjoying her familiar game with a red bath rug and her ball. As always, Maxi won the game, and boy, did that bath rug lose! What a mess of red!

We all piled into the car, but instead of driving to the festival, Ben said to the driver, "Take us to the hospital."

We were dressed for the red carpet—island chic—even Maxi had a little bow around her neck for the occasion. The long hallway leading to the emergency room was bright, but these weren't the bright lights I had hoped for. My face was throbbing and already multicolored.

We didn't have to wait long to see the doctor, and nobody seemed to mind that Maxi was with us. After introducing himself, the doctor looked at me kind of curiously and, motioning toward Ben, I said, "He did it again."

We all laughed. It hurt when I laughed.

After a careful examination and full X-rays of my skull, nose, and eyes, Maxi sat on my lap and licked my bruised face while we waited for the nice doctor to come in with the results. The doctor had only good news—my bruises would be sore, but with the exception of a tiny fracture on my nose that would heal by itself, there was no real damage done.

I said to Ben, "Let's go to the festival."

"Are you sure?"

"Positive."

We arrived only about an hour and a half late for the opening night. We had missed the first film but were there in plenty of time for cocktails before the second movie began. On our way, I had stopped to pick up a pair of large red sunglasses to match my dress and hide my injury.

We walked the red carpet with Maxi leading the way—just the three of us—all alone. Now, with my sunglasses on at nine o'clock at night, I really looked like a Hollywood wife. But the photographers were already inside, so my red-on-red scheme went completely unnoticed. Luckily, so did my battered face.

The first thing we saw when we walked into the courtyard where the ceremonies were held was a large, chiseled ice sculpture in the shape of a dachshund on a marble platform right in the middle of the room. Above the dog, carved in ice, was, "Welcome Ben Gazzara!" and in smaller letters at the base of the sculpture, "and Maxi."

Because we had arrived so late on an already warm evening, the ice sculpture had begun to melt, accumulating puddles of water beneath

the nose and tail. Maxi was quick to remind us that we had neglected our hourly water duty in our haste at the hospital as she lapped up the water from her honorary statue. Maxi's melting really came in handy.

The rest of the night was smoother than the beginning and so was the rest of the festival. I spent the whole week hiding behind my shades. Instead of bringing a nice suntan back to New York, I looked like a prize fighter who'd just lost the bout. I spent what would have been my beach time searching the island for a red bath mat to replace the one Maxi tore up on opening night. Red must have been our cursed color that week. The villa owners had to settle for my sincere apologies because there was no red bath mat to be found on Marco Island.

Germany

*M*AXI AND I are both German; I talk funny and she walks funny. Ben was going to be honored at a film festival in Germany, and for the first time, our little girl was on her way to her homeland. And so was I.

On our way to Bremen, we stopped for a few days in Berlin, which is perhaps the most dog-loving city in Germany with more than a half-million dogs registered and who knows how many others. Our hotel, the elegant Adlon, welcomed Maxi with open arms. When we checked in, a chambermaid came immediately to the lobby with a big cushion and two bowls, one for water and one for food, and a little jar full of cookies with a tag that said, "*Willkommen* Maxi, *zum* Adlon Hotel."

What a treat. Before we left the lobby, the manager pet Maxi and said, "I have one like you at home."

I asked, "How old is your dachshund?"

"Fourteen and healthy as a horse."

"Herr Director, you made my day."

He invited us for a drink later that evening and told us not to worry about keeping Maxi on a leash—she was free to roam the hotel grounds with us.

When we arrived at our lovely suite, I unpacked the luggage while Ben made Maxi comfortable. He found a nice spot for her cushion and put her toys there. And after she ate her dinner, she enjoyed a fine dessert of German doggie cookies. They looked and smelled so delicious, I could have eaten one myself.

It wasn't long before Ben was ready for a nice cold German beer, so I sent him downstairs with Maxi while I got dressed for dinner.

As soon as I was alone in the room, I was taken back to my youth, and I must admit, I was more sentimental than usual. When I was a young girl at just seventeen years old, I began my career as a model in Berlin. At the time, there were two Berlins. I lived in West Berlin, and the Adlon Hotel belonged to East Berlin and was frequented by the most important guests allowed in East Germany. I remembered looking at its elegant facade in my youth and wishing that the world was one place instead of two. To be in the Adlon now was a dream, from a long time ago, come true.

I don't know how long I daydreamed, but sometime later, I joined Ben and Maxi in the bar. Well, I joined Ben at least; Maxi was nowhere in sight. After pretending like he didn't know she was missing for just long enough for me to begin to panic, Ben smiled and pointed to the bartender.

I looked up and saw a familiar and friendly face. It was our favorite bartender from the Palace Hotel in St. Moritz. And there at his feet was Maxi eating peanuts. She was making herself at home in

Germany already and kissing up to the bartender—no doubt hoping for a free drink.

"Congratulations on your new family member. I see you've taught her well. I promise I only gave her water—no beer."

"It's too late. She's incorruptible," Ben said. "Give her a beer if she wants it."

Before I could say anything, Ben laughed out loud and we all joined him. Even Maxi chimed in with her familiar bark.

"*Prost* Maxi, *willkommen* in Berlin," the bartender said with a warm smile.

THE NEXT DAY, while Ben was dubbing some dialogue for a picture, I took Maxi for a walk down the Kurfürstendamm, which is like the Fifth Avenue of Berlin. It was a glorious day in Germany. I reminisced fondly as we strolled this famous street. It was here where I first made my mark and my marks—Deutschmarks. Somehow it seems like a lifetime ago; what memories I had made here. As Maxi and I retraced my steps from years ago toward the first high fashion house where I worked as a girl, we stopped at an outdoor café called Cafe Kranzler to enjoy a nice cool drink and some fascinating people-watching. Berlin for me is like a little New York—a very international and dynamic city. It felt good to be home again—in my first country with my dog—also a German girl.

After our intermission at the café, we continued the three short blocks to the building where I had my first job as a model. It was a very impressive building then and now. Somehow I appreciated its beauty even more this time. Maxi too must have liked what she saw. She couldn't wait to leave her scent right there on the spot. She caught me completely off guard and unprepared when she made a mountain of poop directly in front of the entrance to the landmark building. I wondered if it was possible that she caught my scent here from many moons ago and wanted to leave her own scent behind—her nose is certainly very powerful. It also could have been the pound of peanuts she had stolen from the bar the night before. Either way, I found myself in a very precarious situation with a mountain of poop and no bag, no tissue, no nothing to clean up Maxi's mess.

There were people walking in every direction on the street and coming in and out of the building right in front of my dilemma. Everyone looked at me, watching my next move. I didn't know what to do. The Germans are so particular about cleanliness and order.

Maxi was relieved, but I certainly wasn't. I looked around in agony but didn't know where to turn for help.

Suddenly, a kind man appeared from a bar across the street with some napkins for me. I thanked him with an embrace and cleaned up the sidewalk. It seemed like everywhere we went lately, Maxi had to leave her mark on the way out—even though I see it as a sign of good luck—I think her exits might need work.

WE LEFT BERLIN with one eye smiling and one eye crying—nostalgia is quite an emotion—I was looking forward to the festival in Bremen because it was in another of my favorite parts of Germany—the north—near where I grew up as a little girl. Some members of my family joined us for a long lunch one day, and I enjoyed introducing Maxi to her German relatives.

My younger brother Audi looked at me and said, "Remember when we were young, no animals were allowed at home?"

"Yes," I said, "unfortunately."

"And now all of us have them—it's never too late."

THE WEATHER IN northern Germany was typical for September. It was already too chilly, and it was raining cats and dogs, so when Ben received a phone call that cut our trip short by a day, I wasn't too disappointed. Little did I know that one day would be a very important day.

September 11

$\mathcal{W}$E FLEW BACK to New York City on September 10, 2001.
We arrived in the early afternoon, and it was a gorgeous day.

"Indian Summer," Ben said.

And it was. There are ten perfect days a year in New York City, and this was certainly one of them. We rode back into the city with the windows down, and Maxi had her head out the window while her tail wagged happily inside the car.

The sunny afternoon already felt like evening because we were still on German time. It wasn't long after Maxi's dinner that we all went to bed.

Early to bed, early to rise—even Maxi woke up before the sun. Ben read his *New York Times* while I made breakfast. Maxi did her business on the paper because of the time change. Hoping for another Indian Summer day, Ben promised us a long walk in Central Park and lunch at the Boathouse. While we were unpacking in the den after breakfast, we joined the rest of the world, stunned and horrified, as we witnessed the attacks on the World Trade Center.

Ben, Maxi, and I stood paralyzed in front of the television watching the world change before our very eyes. What an unimaginable day. As fast as things were happening around us, life suddenly went into slow motion. It wasn't long before the fumes and a strange gray dust found their way all the way uptown where we live. The smell was rancid—the dust was everywhere. Maxi was trying hard to figure out the odor. She ran around the apartment sniffing wildly with her fine nose.

There was an eerie feeling looming over the city. No one knew who was responsible for such an awful thing or whether there was more to come. If the point of terrorism is to create terror—they had succeeded. We stayed like prisoners in our own home glued to the news.

For the next couple of weeks, we witnessed firsthand the pain and agony of that day. Our home on Madison Avenue is next door to Campbell's Funeral Home—a well-respected and well-known funeral parlor. The victims' families and friends lined up around our block every day, sometimes two or three times a day, to pay their final respects to their loved ones. Many of them were too young to know death. The firefighters and police officers arrived in large groups to honor their fallen heroes. Mothers and daughters, husbands and sons, grandmothers, uncles, friends, and colleagues, all dressed in black, still stunned by the catastrophe—their faces strewn with empty sorrow—filed by our home for what seemed like an eternity to pay their final respects to loved ones whose bodies were not even found.

When we went for Maxi's daily walks, she was quick to bring a smile to some sad faces. People often caressed her and gave her loving pats, and she always obliged with her happy brown eyes, a firm tail wag, and sometimes even a warm mouthful of kisses. She was tireless with her attention and affection.

Out of respect, Maxi moved her powder room to the next corner.

LESS THAN TEN days after the eleventh, Ben was asked by the NYPD to go down to Ground Zero to meet the workers. They wanted him to bring his famous face and some cheer to the site. He gladly agreed. When the day arrived, a police car came to pick us up, and we barreled through the streets of the city with New York's finest. Maxi and I wanted to join Ben for these potentially heavy moments, but the stench, dust, and fumes from the World Trade Center were still over-powering and too strong. So while Ben signed helmets and T-shirts and carried on nice conversations with the Ground Zero personnel, she and I walked around the perimeter and took in the thousands of flowers, teddy bears, letters, and photographs that had been left as memorials—it was really heartbreaking. There were so many lost lives being remembered, so many tears being shed. Looking around and feeling the loss of these fathers and mothers and sons and daughters, I found myself weeping uncontrollably. I don't know how long I cried. It was a chilling moment. The air was heavy with loss. Maxi too was moved, I could feel it. To this day, I swear she was crying with me. By the time Ben found us for lunch with the captain of the police force, both of our faces were wet with grief. Maybe Maxi was feeling the pain for her fellow canines. There were twenty or more dogs changing shifts as one group entered and one group exited the restricted site with their handlers. In addition to the human victims of 9/11, I wondered how many barking heroes were made martyrs on that fateful morning.

THAT AUTUMN IN New York wasn't like autumn in New York at all. The months passed by slowly. The city was lifeless and sad. The tourists weren't coming. Broadway shows were closing. Shops and hotels were empty. New York was not New York.

For the animals, though, life went on as usual. It always brightened my day to watch the dogs play in the park. That year, Maxi stayed on her leash as we both witnessed the squirrels burying their nuts for the winter, and soon enough, the holidays were upon us.

Still, while the city that never sleeps seemed to be slumbering, I could tell the giant was waking up. The charities were booming. Rock stars, politicians, movie stars, and people from every walk of life volunteered their time, their money, and their love to victims and businesses alike. America had never been more patriotic. I became obsessed with the American flag in the same way I had been obsessed with all things dachshund when we first met Maxi. Little did I know the American flag would launch my next creative adventure.

No Dogs in Dogville

*B*EN'S NEXT LEADING lady was Nicole Kidman, but I wasn't jealous at all because I spent my days with Maxi. About a month before Ben left for Sweden to begin filming *Dogville*, we had lunch in New York with the Swedish producer at the Union Cafe. She had come over for business and wanted to meet with Ben so he could sign contracts.

"Please bring your wife," she said.

Not an unusual request and I was happy to go. I had read the script and enjoyed it, and I was excited for Ben to work on such a great art film. The producer of this outstanding script must be a special lady, I thought, and I looked forward to meeting her.

Maxi joined us, as always, and remained unnoticed in her bag under the table the entire time—well, most of the time. At some point during lunch, I mentioned to Ben quietly that Maxi needed her carrot.

Ben made some hand gestures to the waiter, who had waited on us many times, and within a few minutes, a single carrot arrived on a large silver platter.

"*Voila, pour mademoiselle,*" he said grandly as he presented the platter.

"For my rabbit," Ben said to the producer with a sly smile as he took the carrot from the platter and slipped it under the table to Maxi.

The producer seemed puzzled. "Our dog," I said quickly. "Today a carrot, next month a smorgasbord in Sweden."

"Oh no, oh no," she said, "you can't bring the dog to Sweden."

Ben and I looked at each other with astonishment. "Really?" I asked. "Is there no way to bring her in?"

"No. Unfortunately not."

I couldn't believe my ears. But before he could even think of backing out of the picture, I said, "I have a great idea, Ben. You go to Sweden, and Maxi and I will wait for you in Umbria. It's been a long time since it's been just us girls."

"Lauren Bacall also has a little dog and cannot bring hers either," the producer told us. "She's also very upset."

"Or maybe we could rent a house-boat with Lauren off shore in Sweden where we could live happily with our dogs like Liz Taylor did during *Cleopatra*," I said jokingly. "The film is called *Dogville*, after all."

WELL, IRONIC AS it was, while Ben filmed *Dogville*, Maxi and I stayed in our home in Umbria during an unusually cold winter in Italy. Though the Italian weather was nothing like the freezing weather in the mountains of Sweden, Maxi and I still cuddled up nightly in front of our warm fireplace, and when it was extra cold, I wrapped her in an American flag scarf that I had purchased in New York along with a lot of other patriotic knickknacks before we left America. She loved that scarf. We spent the days lunching with friends and relaxing at home. The nights would have been very lonely except for Franca. She is our housekeeper there, and she often stayed with Maxi and me knitting the nights away while we watched TV together and kept each other company.

It was during one of those very cold Italian nights when Maxi refused to go outside because of the extreme weather that I got my inspiration to become a designer.

A Warm Hug

*M*axi's shivering gave me the idea to have Franca knit a handmade, Italian dog coat for Maxi. When I made the proposal to her, she asked me what kind of coat she should knit. It didn't take me long to regain my own patriotic Americanism and suggest that she make a dog coat with the pattern of an American flag. And that's what she made. But Franca didn't stop with the American flag coat. That coat was just the beginning of a unique dog-coat collection made with love. *Un abbracio caldo*, "A Warm Hug," was born.

Maxi, my glamorous and patient supermodel, was soon the best-dressed girl in town. By the time Ben arrived from Sweden, my collection was almost complete, and I was ready to conquer the market.

When we returned to New York, I nervously smuggled the first coats into the country. I had two entire suitcases filled with little coats. My brain was working constantly to find an excuse in case I had to open my bags at customs. What would I say? Could all of these be

gifts? How many coats could one small dog own after all? Luckily we breezed right through customs, and during our ride into the city, I realized that a huge weight had been lifted from my shoulders. The first batch of "A Warm Hug" had arrived safely in America.

DURING THE NEXT few weeks, Maxi was my walking billboard. Every day we went out, she wore a new creation. Wintertime was dying down in New York, but it was still a very cold March.

Maxi became my muse. She looks adorable dressed in my sweaters and she knows it. When I say, "You are beautiful," in a high-pitched voice, she jumps around until I pick her up and then she fills my face with wet kisses.

But now I was getting nervous. It was time to receive the first delivery of "A Warm Hug," and they hadn't arrived. There was a postal

strike in Italy, but thank God it was a short one. When they finally came, I opened the big box and brought out a few of the sweaters, I was very pleased. They were stunning, but they had a strange odor. I took another handful out of the carton, brought them close to my nose, and I almost laughed out loud. It smelled as though Franca, my top knitter in Umbria, had sent me a prosciutto or a salami and smuggled them between my coats. I dug through the box and there was nothing, only the sweaters and the smell. Then I realized what it was. Franca and her ladies who knit with her usually sit facing a fireplace, and in that room, hanging from large wooden beams, are prosciuttos and salamis in the process of being aged. Maxi was going crazy. Her nose was everywhere. I'd laid out my sweater collection on one of our couches, and she sniffed each one carefully. Right then I realized something unexpected and very special about my sweaters—that smell would help sell!

Maxi and I proudly delivered the new coats to my first customers: Madison Avenue boutiques like Zitomers, Karen, Clearly First, and others. I hoped that the smoky odor would not disturb them. Nobody noticed a thing. They were overjoyed at the great workmanship and the dazzling colors. *Voila!* It was a deal. Maxi was now my supermodel.

She did miss out on one great event though. Once when I was by myself in New York for a couple of days and Maxi was in Sag Harbor with Ben, I arrived home to find an exciting invitation waiting in the mail. It was an invitation from Saks Fifth Avenue to attend the opening of their new pet department. "Come and join us with your dog," it said. I was really excited to go. The invitation was so glamorous, I wished I could be one of their designers, but how could I attend without Maxi, who was my best advertisement?

Then I remembered. I had recently met a charming New York lady at Charles de Gaulle airport in Paris. Her name was Sarah Wolfe, and she owned two miniature shorthaired dachshunds, just like Maxi. I called her and asked her if she'd like to attend the event and let me enter with one of her dogs, pretending it was mine. She was thrilled with the idea, and so we dressed both of the dogs, Gus and Cricket, in my sweaters, and they looked spiffy.

The fifth-floor pet department was filled with elegant ladies and expensive dogs. The press was there filming and photographing the celebrities—Carolina Herrera, Blaine Trump, CeCe Cord, and many more—all showing off their dogs. There was champagne, hors d'oeuvres, and designer dog cookies. A champion dog trainer and a dog psychoanalyst were standing by to answer any and all dog questions.

As we wandered through the room, Sarah and I got a lot of attention. "A Warm Hug" was a hit. I knew I was cheating on Maxi, but business is business. The manager of the entire department came over and asked where we'd found our unique dog sweaters. Well, I wasn't going to let her go, so I moved fast. I told her about my business, that I designed them and had them knitted in a village very near our home in Umbria. She slipped me her business card, and we made an appointment to meet the next day in her office. It looked like I had a new client.

Sicily

*N*OW IT WAS Ben's turn to return to his homeland. Next stop Sicily. Ben's leading lady also had a dog with her, and she warned me on day one that I needed to protect Maxi from Sicilian ticks with a special collar that she had fitted to her dog. She said the Sicilian ticks could be fatal. So, without wasting any time, I found a collar for Maxi from one of only two dog stores in Taormina. I put it around her neck and gave her a kiss knowing that she would be safe, but I was soon concerned that I had saved her too late.

Two nights later, Maxi went into epileptic convulsions. She couldn't sleep and she couldn't stop shaking. I was sure she had been bitten. I searched her whole body for ticks but found none. Still, she was a mess. The whole night was agony. I held her in my arms. Ben and I couldn't figure out what was happening to our little baby. It was Friday night, and there was no vet to be found until Monday. We had three days to nurture a shaking, sleepless, exhausted, and sick Maxi.

Early Monday morning, it was Ben who discovered Maxi's ailment during a stroke of genius. While inspecting her body again, he took off her treated collar and found a small cut underneath it. It was obvious that the medicine from the collar was irritating the cut and entering her bloodstream, affecting her nervous system. The cut was inflamed and swollen. There were no ticks—only the toxic, tick-preventing medicine. We washed the wound and watched Maxi get better and better. Within only a few hours, after three days of restless agitation, Maxi was almost back to normal. That evening, we celebrated Sicilian style—even Maxi devoured her plate of pasta before she passed out from her three-day spell of exhaustion. She recuperated just in time to receive the royal treatment in Morocco, where the movie continued filming in Rabat, the city of the king.

Morocco

*W*HEN WE ARRIVED in Morocco with Maxi, we had a lot of trouble getting her into the country. They have a very strict policy about foreign pets there, and by the time we flew into Casablanca, we had been out of America so long that her paperwork had expired. Fortunately, they were more excited to have Ben in the country than they were upset about having Maxi, so we were allowed entry on the condition that we took Maxi to a Moroccan vet within twenty-four hours.

We took a car about an hour to Rabat and checked into a magnificent hotel. The producer of the film was happy to have us there, and he quickly set about organizing a vet to stamp Maxi's papers. In fact, he sent us to the king's personal vet, who also has a dachshund. We were in good hands.

I had been to Rabat before. Some years earlier, in another lifetime it seems, during a trip to Marrakech, I spent a happy New Year's Eve there with King Hassan, his family, and friends of mine from Germany

who were invited with us because of our shared passion for polo. Now, these many moons later, King Hassan's kind son, the new king of Morocco, invited us to enjoy his private beach anytime with Maxi.

While Ben worked, she and I spent many wonderful hours on that beach. Maxi loved to run along the area where the water meets the sand. It was very hot but very pleasant. There was no humidity—the air was crisp and perfect. We enjoyed lunches together at an amazing seaside restaurant that serves the king and his friends, and even though there wasn't another dog in sight, Maxi made herself right at home. Every guest on that beach knew Maxi. She became a famous beach bum. When we arrived, there was always a large water bowl and Maxi's own special soft chair waiting for us with two umbrellas, one for each of us. It was hard getting us off that beach, but the souks were calling; there were shoes and kaftans to be bought. Maxi joined me on many shopping trips around Rabat. Our driver knew all of the right stores—he must have read my mind because everywhere he took me was right where I wanted to shop!

There was nothing to buy for Maxi. Dog articles are not in demand in Morocco. But soon, every shopkeeper knew Maxi. When we arrived in the morning, the shopkeepers came running to our car saying, "Maxi, Maxi." I had Moroccan tea while she played with those lovely people in several shops during the day. In fact, I still have a unique dachshund handbag that I co-created with one of the shops in Rabat. Maxi's face is embroidered on the side of a burgundy leather bag. Each day, Maxi and I would stop by for tea and playtime, the young owner and I discussed the design. He presented it to me before we left and it is truly one of a kind. There is even a real collar on the bag around her neck with a heart-shaped dog tag that says, "Maxi." Whenever I carry the handbag, I am reminded of our happy time in colorful Morocco.

The days were delightful, but the nights were a different matter; Morocco is enchanting at night. We replaced the mint teas with flowing wine, couscous, Middle Eastern music, and belly dancing. Maxi enjoyed the music, too, and she was also happy to replace her nightly pasta with this new couscous. But her favorite thing was to watch those belly dancers. I guess she loved the music, the exotic environment, and all of those bells. Even during my private belly dancing lesson in our hotel suite, Maxi never barked or made a noise during the dancing. She would just lie there on a big Moroccan cushion and watch from start to finish. As a reward after each lesson, I took her in my arms and danced the last dance with her. Not quite Ginger and Fred, but we shook it up a little bit and made some nice moves.

One day, Ben cut my dancing lesson short. He arrived at the hotel, home early from shooting, with a dilemma. He had lost a crown, and the king's dentist was the best solution for a new one. Funny, for a country that was so difficult about letting Maxi in, suddenly our baby had carte blanch and was free to join us almost everywhere. During Ben's entire dental procedure, Maxi sat on his belly watching over every move that dentist made. Even though he had to pause often to

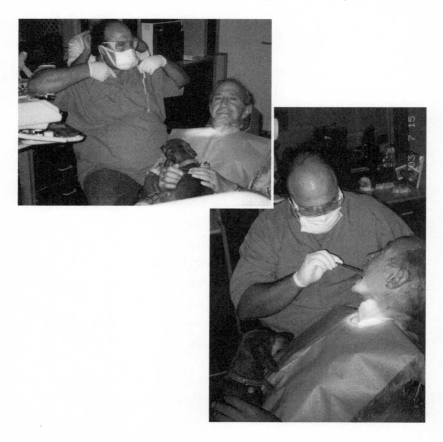

laugh because he had never had a dog in his dental chair before, fittingly, the king's dentist in Morocco gave Ben one of the best crowns he's ever had—another noble treatment.

When the film wrapped in Rabat, it was hard to say good-bye to Morocco. But we were on our way to another royal engagement—next stop Monte Carlo.

Monaco

*I*T WAS EASY entering France with Maxi. They love dogs there. We had been invited by our friend Ruda Dauphin to a very prestigious writer's festival where we got to meet and make friends with Russell Banks, William Kennedy, and Mary Higgins Clark—what superb company. We spent delicious spring days in the sunshine enjoying the French food and sultry French evenings celebrating the exhilarating Monte Carlo nightlife. Maxi was a high roller, and she only rolled with the best—welcome everywhere we went both day and night. She didn't win much—but she didn't bet much either.

We ate at the finest restaurants in and out of town—it was a real treat. Maxi was very keen on the five-star cuisine. She became a real connoisseur. Lamb and duck were her new favorites. Often, when we left the restaurant, Russell Banks would carry Maxi inside of her case all the way to the splendid Hotel Hermitage, where we

were all staying. I think he was smitten. I'm sure his next dog will be a dachshund.

And then the fun really began. We would gather in the hotel bar, Maxi included, for our famous nightcaps. There was always interesting and amusing conversation. I remember with pleasure sitting one night next to the fine writer Mary Higgins Clark and her lovely daughter having a chat about *bella Italia* when Maxi poked her head out of her bag and looked at us curiously. She seemed very interested in our girl talk. Russell Banks lifted her up and put her on his lap. "You are all mine Maxi. Come to visit me in Miami. We'll go fishing together."

Maxi's tail started to wag. She was accepting the invitation.

DURING ONE OF the festival's black-tie events, we were honored with the presence of Prince Albert. In fact, we were seated next to him at dinner, and Maxi sat at our feet. He was a charming man. I'm not sure he ever knew what was in that bag by our feet. I saw him looking under the table often, wondering what may be going on under there, but he never asked and we never told. I still wonder if he thought I was crazy. I talked several times to Maxi under the table. I don't know who he thought I was talking to, but he always nodded politely, and we continued dinner and even danced with the Brazilian band. At one point, I saw from afar that Maxi's bag was shaking— probably she was dancing, too—the samba is one of her favorite dances.

On our way back to the hotel that evening, I said to Ben, "I wonder what Maxi was thinking under that table for so long."

"She must have been saying to herself, 'When the heck are we getting out of here. I'm tired of looking at shoes. I want to go home and play with my ball.' "

"Those were some royal shoes, Ben."

"I want to go home to *my* bed."

"You are both getting too old."

I could have danced all night.

Bilbao

_F_RANK GEHRY AND Ben have been friends since the mid-sixties. When Frank's masterpiece, the Guggenheim Museum in Bilbao, Spain, was completed in 1997, we were invited to the grand opening, but we were on the other side of the world. A few years went by and Ben called Frank from Italy saying that we intended to finally get over to Bilbao. Frank insisted that we postpone until he could be with us. And so more years passed, and in September of 2005, the San Sebastian Film Festival honored Ben with a Lifetime Achievement Award.

We were so close to Bilbao that Ben reached Frank and told him of our intentions. We were finally going to see his masterwork. When we arrived, the museum director himself met us at the entrance to the building. I began to put Maxi into a carrying case, but the gentleman said with a wink, "Your dog has been cleared for entrance." So Maxi had the first museum tour given to a dog.

I held firmly onto her leash as we walked through Richard Serra's iron maze, "The Matter of Time," examined the Robert Rauschenberg paintings, scanned the Lichtensteins, and looked at the Andy Warhols. What an eclectic mix of art they had, funny and smart.

LUNCH WAS WAITING for us in the private dining room whose walls, tables, and chairs were also designed by Frank. The food was superb; the service friendly and cheerful. Frank had really set us up. Maxi, who waited patiently in her case under the table, was rewarded occasionally with a piece of raw carrot. When we got outside, we were thrilled to see an enormous dog made of cut flowers standing at the exit. It had been created by the artist Jeff Koons, and it stood two stories tall. And we still don't know when and if they change the flowers. Are they artificial? Are they real? We should ask Frank.

Maxi & Monk

W E ENDED UP spending a very relaxing and warm summer in Europe. It was one of those rare, enjoyable times in life when pool-side lunches blend into starlit dinners, and there is more than enough time to stop and smell the flowers. We took day trips to Assisi and Florence and spent some weekends with our friends in Tuscany who had an adorable little dog named Monk. Maxi and Monk were jetsetter friends—they played together everywhere from Palm Beach to Umbria and from Tuscany to Sag Harbor. I often wondered when I saw them together what dogs must think of their dog friends. What must it be like for a dog to suddenly see an old friend halfway around the world and pick up right where they had left off, as if they'd never been apart?

Every time Maxi and Monk met, their greetings followed the same pattern. After some licks and sniffs and plenty of wagging, Monk would lead Maxi to his toy box and bring each of his toys out for Maxi to play

with—generously placing them one by one right at her feet. I never grew tired of watching that routine. They had a beautiful friendship.

When we arrived in Tuscany, we were happy to see our friends, but the magic was missing once Monk died. He lived to be thirteen. He was happy and healthy until the end when he died peacefully in his sleep.

Maxi was puzzled and looked everywhere for him. She must have thought he was hiding from her, playing one of their innocent games. Maxi acted as if she expected Monk to appear from around the corner any moment. She searched and searched for her friend. The best she could find was a rubber shoe that had been lost behind a bush near the pool house. Mimicking her old game with Monk, but playing a different part, Maxi brought Monk's toy and placed it at my feet. Ben and I were moved.

During lunch, our friends told us how they helped each other through the difficult moments of their pet's death and about the touching funeral they gave Monk up on his favorite hill. They said they often brought fresh flowers to Monk's grave and would spend a few minutes there remembering the spirit of their baby. Soon we were all in tears.

After lunch, while everyone else went for siesta, I took Maxi for a walk up the hill. It was an enchanting walk. There were ancient olive trees everywhere and a carpet of roses. This had been one of their favorite hills to play on. Now I could see why. And when I saw the tombstone, I knew the reason they had chosen this spot. It was a little piece of heaven on Earth, stunning from every angle. They had created a peaceful garden around the grave site, and there was a stone bench nestled between the pine trees, a perfect place to sit and collect my thoughts and say a prayer.

Maxi ran right up to the grave and found a place in the sun, next to her old friend. I looked at her standing there looking back at me with her eyes squinting from the sun, and I thanked God for my little girl. I prayed earnestly for a long and healthy life for her, for Ben, and for myself. I prayed for my friends, who I knew were grieving over their loss. And I prayed for Monk, whose spirit was still so strong, I could feel him smiling down on us from dog heaven. I wondered if Maxi was somehow also saying good-bye to her friend. We stayed up on the hill for a while, and as we walked down together, I remember feeling a deep sense of inner peace.

Maxi & Lilly

LUCKY FOR MAXI—and for us too—we were heading straight from those heavy moments in Tuscany to visit our friends Aristela and Sergio and Maxi's friend Lilly on their luxury yacht for a weeklong private cruise on the Côte d'Azur. Aristela and I have been friends for many years. Sergio, her husband of forty years, is a sweet but tough cookie and is very proud of his 65-meter yacht. He is also very particular about who he invites on board. But when he saw how well Maxi and Lilly got along at their house on the lake in Lugano, Switzerland, he said to Aristella, "Look at Maxi. What life, what personality."

Then he invited us with our baby to join him on his baby, *The Lady Marina*.

So Maxi, Ben, and I joined them and a group of their close friends on a spectacular cruise in the South of France. Maxi was happy to be with Lilly again. She was the first and perhaps only dog Maxi did not

bark at when they first met. She was comfortable in Lilly's company from the beginning; they wined and dined and enjoyed each other in complete harmony. Lilly would often playfully nip at Maxi's chubby paws and Maxi allowed her to have her fun.

At each port of call, Maxi walked with me on the boulevards in Nice and Cap Ferrat; she even showed herself off in lively Saint Tropez. Lilly and Aristela were always close behind. We each had a jetsetter on our hand.

Our days and nights on the yacht were full of fun. We ate, we drank, we swam in the sea and in the pool, we danced, we laughed, and then did it all over again day after day. It was a pleasure to sail

with our dozen or so close friends. Maxi was happy to have her friend along, too, and they often entertained themselves for hours without checking in with us. Those two dogs were the real captains of the ship. They had all-access passes, and Maxi's hunting instincts took them to every corner of the boat. My biggest fear was that Maxi would do her duty on one of the many expensive white rugs covering the fine floors on Sergio's enormous luxury yacht. But Maxi controlled herself. It was as though she knew that if she had an accident, she would really be in the doghouse.

They spent many hours playing on the long decks of the yacht chasing the ball while we were at sail in the Mediterranean. Sometimes under the sun and sometimes under the full moon, she mastered her game and entertained herself and often Lilly, too. We could hear them barking and playing sometimes two decks away— clear across the boat—and we knew they were safe and happy and probably out of trouble.

One evening, however, trouble arrived. The full moon was shining brightly above the sea and everyone was out on deck dancing and enjoying after-dinner drinks when Aristela discreetly tapped me on my shoulder. I turned around and instinctively followed her silently as she led me toward her master suite. This was a stunning room full of antiques, rugs, paintings, and other objects each more valuable than many people's entire homes. From floor to ceiling, the suite is unbe-lievably beautiful.

Still without a word, Aristela looked toward the equally exquisite marble bathroom and I knew instantly—without even looking—why she'd brought me here. I could only pray that for some unknown rea-son, they'd bought their bath rug at Bed Bath & Beyond. But, it wasn't that simple. Aristela calmly walked to the bathroom and opened the door. Maxi and Lilly ran out of the bathroom like two little sinners. Maxi's face was full of white fuzz and string. There was nothing on little Lilly's face.

I knew what I would see, but still, I wasn't prepared for this. The bathroom was a battlefield full of what looked like shredded white cotton—unfortunately, it was shredded white *antique silk*. Mama Mia, I couldn't believe my eyes. It wasn't the biggest mess Maxi had ever made, but it was certainly the most expensive. Where would I possibly find a replacement for this rug?

Nervously, I turned to Aristela. We both looked down at Maxi, clearly the culprit, looking more like a sheep than a dog because she was covered in so much white fuzz. Then we both burst out into uncontrollable laughter. We laughed so hard that even Maxi chimed in with her "I love you, I love you, I love you." It was hard to be mad at such an unbelievable but adorable sight. Thank goodness my friend Aristela was such a good sport. I guess that's one of the reasons our friendship has lasted so long.

We both got on our hands and knees in our evening dresses and collected all of the shredded and torn silk from the floor and returned to the party as if nothing had happened.

Later that evening, I had a private chuckle when I pulled some stray pieces of white silk bath rug from Aristela's hand-beaded dress. I don't know what she told Sergio because he still loves Maxi. I never mentioned to either of them that bath rugs are Maxi's specialty.

Umbria—
Summer's End

*A*S YOU CAN see, Maxi has a lot of friends. Vincent Crapanzano and his wife Jane Kramer had replaced a dog they had lost with their pet's spitting image. It was a big beauty of a Bouvier des Flandres, which are known for their herding instincts. As soon as Ulie saw Maxi, she decided that the little animal must be protected. When Maxi wandered a bit too far, Ulie would circle her and lead her gently back to us. Maxi seemed to enjoy the game; she always came back smiling. I guess Maxi is a lot like me; we both enjoy being with a girlfriend!

A LOT OF HER friends are in Orvieto, all adopted by my friend Tess Serrante. Maxi's favorite is Isabella, a Chihuahua. But her very best friend is Foxy, a wild, adorable dog who appeared one day at our friend's exquisite Umbrian castle, circling it for days. They placed food for him far away from their home. In time, they brought it closer and closer. Slowly and carefully, Foxy followed his food until the time came

when his bowl was placed at the feet of our friends who were seated on their splendid terrace having cocktails and watching the stunning evening sky. Joe Hellman, our friend, looked to his wife Ursula and she nodded; it was time to attempt to touch the wild dog. As soon as Foxy finished his food, Joe reached down, ever so slowly, and pet his head. Foxy didn't move. And so, Joe caressed him and, in return, Foxy gave Joe a broad lick and that was that. The Hellmans had a new family member.

Maxi was not a big fan of Foxy's. The first time she met Foxy, *he* was very civilized, but Maxi barked endlessly from inside her bag, disrupting our time with the Hellmans. We decided that if we let her out of her carrying case, the two sweet animals would get used to each other better. It was a miracle. First they walked side by side and then they started running and playfully chasing each other. I even think I saw them hugging. Foxy is a handsome devil and Maxi is no fool. The girl in her took over.

Maxi gets especially excited when we visit our friends at their castle in Torregentile, which is also quite near to us. The warm inviting cantina where we have drinks and dinner is not only full of enormous wooden wine barrels, but also has many salamis, prosciuttos, and cheeses hanging from the arched ceilings. A few times, I saw Maxi looking up to the ceiling. I knew she was thinking and planning, "How the hell do I get near enough to one of those salamis, prosciuttos, or whatever without being noticed?"

But she knew that would take magic, so she turned away from the source of her temptation, in search of her squeaky ball. Maxi always adapts to any new situation.

Back to New York

*A*FTER AN AMAZING summer, it was time to go home to New York. Work was calling, there were business meetings, and most importantly, Ben needed some quiet time to continue writing his memoirs and also to prepare for an upcoming play.

It had been a year since 9/11 and the city was still in mourning. We were invited by Patty Lynch, the head of the police union, to the event honoring the wives and children of the police and firemen who lost their lives on that dreadful day one year before. On the way downtown, we stopped the car at Ground Zero and told the driver to wait. Even though we had been there before, I found myself caught up in the grief as though it was the first time. I could tell we had quite a night of heavy emotions ahead of us.

When we arrived, we saw immediately that the majority of guests were women and children—the wives, daughters, and other family of the fallen heroes. With food and drinks, lots of ice cream, balloons,

music, and some clowns to make the children laugh, the organizers had worked very hard to make a happy party. Still, the laughter was scarce and the joy seemed to be make-believe. But I must say, those people were determined to go on.

Patty Lynch made a touching speech about the heroic ones who were lost to us. The new mayor, Michael Bloomberg, talked about New York's brave spirit. Ben was asked to pose for many photos. We took Maxi out of her bag and then the cameras really started clicking. There were many pictures taken, including one with Maxi, Mayor Bloomberg, Patty Lynch, and me. We smiled for the photos through our tears for these broken families all around us.

Maxi was at her best. She played with the children like it was a performance, giving those children more fun than the clowns did. I was proud of my little social worker.

WE SPENT THE next few months and the first half of the next year back and forth between New York and Sag Harbor. While Ben was absorbed in his work, Maxi and I were absorbed with ours. The fall and winter months are the perfect months for Maxi to model my new collection. Once again, she played her part to the hilt everywhere we went.

She pranced around Madison Avenue in Manhattan and Main Street in Sag Harbor wearing "A Warm Hug." We shopped together and talked to many friendly strangers about what a beautiful dog Maxi is, and even better, the conversations always led to my hand-knit Italian dog sweaters and how well dressed she was. Not to brag, but wherever we went, she was always the best-dressed girl in town. I was a proud mother and a proud designer! We sometimes coordinated our fashion as a family and supported animal rights and shelters at several key charity events where I was able to donate some "warm hugs" to needy dogs. By Christmastime, "A Warm Hug" was for sale all over the Hamptons. And Maxi was the new famous face behind my new line.

CHRISTMAS BROUGHT the city back to life. The streets, the shops, the hotels, the bars, the restaurants were all full of people and business was booming again. New York was festive and fun, and Ben and I spent nearly every evening out on the town when we were there. We hired a German nanny to sit with Maxi some nights when Ben and I stepped out alone. Maria and Maxi sat together in the den for hours watching television. I don't know what her taste in TV is, but Maxi must have been just so happy to watch something besides Ben's sports. Sometimes when we arrived home, they were both sleeping soundly on the couch. But Maxi's favorite nanny is our friend Lynn. She is not only a big dog lover, but she also has an elegant apartment as big as a football field. For Maxi, life with Auntie Lynn is like Club Med.

AS NICE AS it was to be in New York, that season I preferred our long stays in Sag Harbor. There were high snows, cold nights, and warm fires. Maxi jumped into the snow like a baby kangaroo reminding me

every time of her first visit here when she was a little girl before she was even our dog. Now, years later, she is welcome everywhere like a native.

Sag Harbor has a first-class movie house, but its theater is the star. The Bay Street Theater is run by Cybil Christopher, who was once married to Richard Burton; Emma Walton, the daughter of Julie Andrews; and the extraordinary set designer Tony Walton. Cybil called Ben and told him that she would be delighted to mount a production of *Nobody Don't Like Yogi*, a one-man show about the life and times of Yogi Berra, the legendary New York Yankee. Ben had been interested in the project for more than a year, and he was pleased when the producer, Don Gregory, came on board and started to make things happen.

The rehearsal period was about four weeks, so that gave us an extended period to enjoy our home and little town. Ben would always leave in the mornings for rehearsal, and Maxi and I would spend quiet mornings together with a cozy breakfast and plenty of time for her to play outside. Her new play area and outdoor bathroom was an empty crawl space under the new guest room addition we had built the previous year. It was almost completely covered over with thick green bushes, and I think she must have really enjoyed digging and hiding out there. She would disappear under the house for what seemed like hours. But I knew she was having fun and was probably out of trouble, so I took the opportunity to prepare for the day and I let her play. This went on every day. Her hiding place was her new favorite thing.

Maxi and I also made it a ritual to stroll through the little village to meet Ben for lunch at the small beach across from the Bay Street Theater. The village and beach were quiet because the tourists had not yet invaded.

Each day, I packed a picnic lunch with fresh roasted chicken or delicious sandwiches and fresh fruit. There would always be a bottle of chilled white wine, Maxi's carrot, and her ball, which she never tired of pushing with her nose up and down the beach.

She also started her own ritual with Ben. Before I even got our lunch unpacked, Maxi had devoured her carrot and was ready for action. Every day, it was the same. As soon as she finished eating, she sped like a bullet with her ball toward the ocean, pushing it faster and faster until the ball flew into the water. She's not a swimmer and waves are not her favorite. She would walk into the water two inches up to her knees, but the ball was always far from her reach.

Ben had to roll up his pant legs and walk into the cold water to retrieve it for her. As soon as Ben returned to our table, Maxi was wading in the ocean again expecting a kind wave to bring back her ball. It rarely happened, so Ben had to go again. This went on a few times each day before Ben said, "You go, this time it's your turn."

But he always went. I think he liked having his own game with her.

BEN'S REHEARSAL ENDED each day at 6:00 P.M. Maxi and I often waited for him on the terrace of the American Hotel, which is nearby the theater. We enjoyed pre-dinner cocktails while Maxi had her bowl of water, and if we had dinner out, Maxi's food was always ready and waiting in my handbag.

One night on our way home, Ben said he was particularly tired. He wanted to sleep in the other bedroom so he could hopefully get a good night's sleep. Maxi followed him. I checked on them only ten minutes later, and they were sound asleep. Maxi had her head on the pillow next to Ben's. Adorable. I sat in my bed and I read myself to sleep. It was so quiet and peaceful. After dozing off several times, I turned off the lights and quickly fell asleep.

I don't know how long I slept, but I was suddenly awakened with a loud stomping sound coming from the ceiling. It sounded like the same noise I had heard many times before, but this time, it was even more intense, and it was right above my head. There was something or someone above my bedroom moving and jumping. The fan hanging from the ceiling was shaking, and I became frightened. What the hell was going on?

Maxi woke up and started barking. Ben rushed into my room. "Holy Christ," he said, "did you hear those noises?"

Maxi would not stop barking. She ran from room to room and seemed very nervous and even protective. I had never seen her like this before.

"What could that be Ben?"

"I don't know."

"It could be those big, crazy cats from across the street," I said.

"Cats on a hot tin roof?" He said with a grin as he turned around and headed back to his room saying, "Let's try to get some sleep." Maxi followed him.

I couldn't fall back asleep, but I know they did because I heard Ben's familiar snore all the way down the hall and was sure Maxi was snoring with him. Finally, I dozed off again only to be awakened by a loud human-like scream. It was followed quickly by more ceiling-shaking thumps.

Ben called from the other room, "Holy cow, look at this."

I rushed in and saw that the vent from the air conditioner had fallen from the wall above his bed—it had obviously been pushed by something or someone. There was dust or soot all over the room. We hadn't had an earthquake and I don't believe in ghosts, so what could it be?

"Ben, what's going on?"

"I don't know, this is a puzzle to me."

We called the police.

They arrived with flashlights and had their guns drawn as they approached our house. They looked everywhere. They checked the roof, they looked in the pool, they searched behind every tree.

Finally after nearly twenty minutes of four policemen searching for these terrible noise makers, an officer came into the living room and said, "The good news is there is nobody here. The bad news is I think you might have raccoons. Probably with all of the commotion, they're gone for the rest of the night. Get some sleep and take care of it tomorrow." Before he left, he put a business card on the counter for Gentle Jim and his wife Gentle Jane, "The Best Raccoon Catchers on the North Shore."

THE REST OF the night passed without incident. Somehow we all fell asleep and there were no more noises, so we woke up with the sun, almost refreshed.

First thing that morning, we phoned the Gentles. They came within an hour, sized up the situation, and soon showed us where our problem was. Right in front of the house, up high near the roof, where some tree branches touched the house, there was a huge hole that led straight to the attic. The mystery was solved.

Based on his experience, Gentle Jim guessed that there were at least six or seven raccoons living in our attic, a whole family, all rent free, and for some time. With spring approaching, Jim noted that it was mating season and said that the screams we'd heard the night before were probably the raccoons above us having rough sex—something they are known for—biting and clawing at each other until they are both bleeding.

I remembered those screams and couldn't imagine them coming from a pleasurable act.

I was surprised at what he showed us next. Apparently, Maxi's favorite new hiding place under the new guest addition was the raccoons' playground at night. He brought us around to the side of the house and shined his flashlight through the bushes and showed us their den. I couldn't imagine what Maxi liked about playing in there—except that she is a dog after all; the stench coming from behind those bushes was just awful.

After some explanations and preparations, Gentle Jim and Gentle Jane went about their work. They put up four iron cages right in front of our house with bacon and honey in them. They also put up cages in the backyard and in that smelly animal playpen under the guest room.

Jim told us to keep Maxi inside as much as possible for the next few days while he caught the little creatures. He said she should particularly be kept away from her favorite place behind those bushes—not just because of the traps, but also because of the raccoons.

"She's drawn there because of the odor of the raccoons. But you were lucky; they would have eaten her alive. She must have some guts, your little girl."

Proudly, I said, "Yes, she is a tough hunting dog."

"That wouldn't help her against raccoons. Thank God they sleep during the day. Take care and we'll see you in the morning." With that, they left and there was not much to do but wait. We went on with our day.

Maxi and I met Ben for lunch. I checked every cage when I got back to the house that afternoon. Nothing. Before dinner, I checked again and after dinner too. Still nothing.

We went to sleep that night not knowing what to expect. Maxi was on alert. She knew there were other animals literally in the house. I wondered what the morning might bring.

Ben, Maxi, and I all woke up early, excited by what we might find. We dressed right away and took Maxi with us out front. I held her closely in my arms. Quietly, as if we might disturb them, we crept onto the lawn in the high snow and saw that there was a large raccoon in each of the four cages. I couldn't believe how unnaturally large they were, even more, I couldn't believe how beautiful they were.

For the next three days, we woke up every morning to Gentle Jim and Gentle Jane and they carefully captured the entire family one by one. On the second night, even though they had caught her already, they left the one they thought might be the mother of the missing baby raccoons in her cage on our front lawn overnight. I could hardly take it. I said to Ben, "Let's take the cage in overnight."

He said, "Are you crazy? She would eat all of us."

I went outside just before dark to get a good look at her and make sure she had something to eat for the night. For the first time, it was just

the two of us, and I was truly amazed by her beauty. No makeup artist could have painted her face with a more stunning look, especially the eyes. I made my peace with her and went inside for the night.

Their plan worked. The next morning when we woke up, there were two little raccoons in their separate cages, and finally, the whole family was caught. As they brought the cages closer together, I saw the mother reach out her paw as if to touch one of the babies—her child also reached out for its mother, and it broke my heart.

Gentle Jane saw me crying and quickly came over to comfort me. She told me that the other raccoons had been relocated and dropped off about forty miles away, and she promised me that this mother and her children would stay together and start their new life with the rest of their family.

"I miss them already."

"Don't miss them too much, they might be back."

Before they left, they put a veil over the hole leading into our attic and into Maxi's favorite space behind the bushes. They told us that if the veil remained untouched for the next couple of days, the family was all gone.

It turned out the family was gone, but that was the easy part. It took some weeks to renovate and repair their penthouse and Maxi's favorite place was no longer her favorite place. The wild perfume was gone.

BEN OPENED HIS play with a big success for a two-week engagement, and it was a dream to have him working so near to our little home that meant so much to us. Maxi and I attended almost every performance. We joined Ben backstage before each show, and we were always the first fans to rush his dressing room afterward. His performance was fantastic, and by the end of that short run, I imagine Maxi could have been his understudy. She sat quietly in her bag watching him for ninety minutes, never barking, always listening to make sure her daddy was doing a good job. It was Ben's first time back on stage since his cancer operation, and as soon as Maxi was satisfied with the strength of his performance each night, she slipped off to sleep. The only time she made a sound was at the very end of the show during the ovation and thundering applause. She offered her cheerful barks as her approval. And I gladly let her.

AFTER A VERY successful run in Syracuse, the show was going to open Off-Broadway. We had a few weeks before the New York production began rehearsing when we were invited to the Emmy Awards. Ben was nominated for his performance with Gena Rowlands in *Hysterical Blindness*. I really wanted to go and often imagined us walking the red carpet with Maxi leading the way. I was looking forward to such a glamorous night and even thought how wonderful it would feel to be in the audience if Ben won the award. Maxi would bark, everyone would laugh. Ben would get some well-deserved recognition, and I would be a happy Hollywood wife, for just one night. But no such luck. I married the wrong man. Not one to go to award shows, Ben was content to sit in Sag Harbor and watch his sports on the fateful Sunday night, while he cooked us a tasty plate of pasta *alla puttanesca*.

SO, I TRADED my Gucci gown for a pair of comfortable blue jeans and sat with Maxi upstairs, watching the entire show while Ben called out dinner updates from downstairs almost too often.

Half an hour or so into the live broadcast from Los Angles, I don't remember who heard Ben's name first, me or Maxi; she barked, I screamed, or I screamed and she barked—either way, we must have made a lot of noise. Ben thought the raccoons were back. He came charging up the stairs like a man half his age and found Maxi and I jumping up and down in tears in front of the television. Ben won the Emmy.

Maxi Off-Broadway

*N*OBODY DON'T LIKE *Yogi* opened in October 2003 at the Lamb's Theater, an Off-Broadway house smack in the middle of New York's theater district. The play received good reviews and ran for four months. On matinee days, Maxi and I would join Ben for an early dinner between shows. There was a restaurant across from the theater, which became our home away from home. The management was dog-friendly, and allowed Maxi to sit with us in our favorite corner booth and enjoy her food while we had ours.

Maxi and I would often stay and see the second show. I always chose the mezzanine because it had an occasional empty seat and I could place Maxi in her carrying case on the floor, where she would be next to me and I could keep an eye on her. But on one occasion, near the end of the play, I looked down and Maxi was not there. I left my seat and walked up and down the aisles of the mezzanine peering into row after row. She was nowhere to be found. By this time, the

show was over, and the people around me figured out what was happening and joined in the search. I was becoming more and more frightened and desperate. I never thought I could lose her that way. We'd been to the theater so often and her bag was always open, but she never wandered off. I did not know what to do.

I was beside myself. As I found my way to Ben's dressing room, carrying Maxi's empty bag, I tried to think of things I would say. How would Ben react? I opened the door and, crying hysterically, I said, "I've lost her Ben. She is gone."

Ben seemed bewildered as he looked up at me. "What?" he asked. "You lost who?"

Before I could explain, I looked down and saw Maxi playing with her ball under Ben's costume rack between the shoes and the T-shirts. What was going on? How had she gotten backstage?

"Ben, where did you find her?"

"What do you mean, where did I find her? She found me. Maxi has a hunting dog's nose. She sniffed her way to my dressing room."

Ben then reached down, picked Maxi up, and rocked her in his arms saying, "You love your daddy, don't you Maxi?"

I still can't figure out how she got to that dressing room unnoticed and without crossing the stage.

Maxi & Alexander

*T*HE PREVIOUS SUMMER while we were in Europe, Danja married a young man named Savva, who was born in Russia. She soon became pregnant and gave birth to an adorable baby boy, who has blonde hair and blue eyes. Ben and I invited them to spend a few weeks with us in Sag Harbor.

Only a month before, the three of us—Ben, Maxi, and me—drove into town. Traffic was thick up and down Main Street, and every parking space was taken.

"I'm getting nervous, the town is changing," said Ben.

"It's not the country anymore."

"Why don't we sell our place?"

"Do you really want to?" I asked.

He stopped the car, turned to me, and, with a very serious look, said, "Yes."

Well, that was it. We got ourselves a broker who quickly found a

buyer who really wanted the house. We would close the deal during my daughter's visit. As that day got closer, my doubts became stronger and stronger. Did I really want to give up the house that held so much of our history?

"It will give us more time to spend in Italy," Ben said.

I thought about that and how happy I always am in Umbria.

"You're right," I said. "Sag Harbor is over. It's no longer the small town we first came to, and most of our friends have died or gone away."

WHEN I OPENED the door, there they were. Danja was holding an eight-month-old baby boy who chuckled when he saw me. I felt like I'd seen him before.

"Mommy, this is Alexander," she said, lovingly placing him in my arms.

"It's good to see you again, Mrs. Gazzara," said her husband, whom we had not seen since before their wedding.

"Please call me Elke."

As I held that lovely little boy, I realized who he reminded me of. Me. In my baby pictures, I have the same blonde hair, the same blue eyes, and the same full, round cheeks. I kissed Alexander again and again. Maxi was behind us standing on her hind legs barking. I think she was jealous.

We spent most of our days together around the swimming pool. Alexander sat in an inflatable chair with Savva pushing from behind, and Maxi had her own chair, which I pushed. Then, sitting on the deck, Danja helped Alexander toss Maxi's ball so that she would retrieve it and bring it back to them. The baby was delighted with the game and with Maxi. They were becoming fast friends.

For one lunch, Ben had made a pasta alla puttanesca. Maxi was excited because she knew she'd get some too. Savva and Danja liked the pasta, but Alexander was overjoyed. He needed no fork. He used his hands, happily picking strands of spaghetti from his bowl, eating some with his toothless mouth and dropping a good deal on the floor, which Maxi happily vacuumed. When the meal was over, the floor was spotless.

On many afternoons, Danja would take Alexander up to the den to view cartoons called *Baby Mozart, Baby Bach*, and *Baby Beethoven* that contained children, animals, toys, and classical music. Alexander would watch and laugh. Maxi placed herself right at the edge of his blanket. She was being protective and would not allow anything bad to happen to her new friend.

The two weeks came to an end too quickly, and as Danja and Savva took Alexander to New York to prepare for his christening, we prepared to leave our precious home. I sent Ben to book a room at the American Hotel where our journey to Sag Harbor first began. We had stayed there often while our house was being built. And now it was almost time to go. It was time to say good-bye.

While three strong-looking guys moved couches, chairs, tables, and TV sets, which were given to charity, Maxi and I walked around our grounds for the last time looking at the roses, the lilacs, the jasmine, the forsythia, and the cherry trees. We had planted them all, and it

was very hard to leave them. When the moving men had gone, I climbed the three steps leading to the house. Maxi followed. We looked at the empty interior for a long time. All that was left were the light fixtures and Maxi's food and water bowls. I looked down at Maxi and said, "I think that's enough, Maxi, time to go."

I attached her leash and we left the house. I didn't look back, but Maxi stopped. She didn't want to go any further. Her shining black eyes looked up to me, and that brought tears to mine. I'm convinced that Maxi knew somehow she would never return to the house where she grew up and had always had so much fun.

Book Parties

$\mathcal{B}$EN PUBLISHED HIS memoirs, *In the Moment,* and our friends across the country lined up to throw book parties. Lee Mellis and his wife Young Hi gave a terrific party in New York. Michael and Karen Ansari opened their elegant home in West Virginia and invited some of the most important people in Washington. In Beverly Hills, our friends and neighbors in Umbria, Merle and Peter Mullen, gave us an exquisite dinner party where, unfortunately, Maxi left her calling card. They made no fuss about it because they too love our little girl. And then another book party in Dallas where Robert and Myrna Schlegel invited their good friends to their wonderful home. It was my first time in Dallas, and it was Maxi's first time, too.

When the time came for the event, the expansive home was filled with more than 200 people drinking champagne and enjoying the delicious canapés. Myrna placed Ben in the lush, comfortable den and seated him at an antique desk next to hundreds of copies of his book.

He was there to chat with each and every guest and sign a copy of his book for them.

Maxi kept Ben company sitting lazily on his lap but absorbing every moment. The people would wander in and make some small talk while getting their books signed. One sharply dressed and attractive lady with a bubbly personality came toward Ben with a glass of champagne in one hand and picked up a book with the other. Ben signed it, and as he rose to hand it to her, she bent over to kiss him on the cheek. Big mistake! She shouldn't have done that because the ferocious protector came out of Maxi. She sprang up, growled, and let out one of her loudest barks ever. The lady was so shocked that she threw her champagne in the air, and it spilled all over her magnificent silk dress. Thank God she had a sense of humor. "Luckily your dog is not a rottweiler—I thought she was going to tear my face off!" she remarked.

At full speed, I ran over to her with all of the napkins I could find. "Please forgive her. Maxi is the jealous type."

"Are you sure you didn't *train* her to attack?" asked the lady.

Everybody laughed—actually it was a funny start to a great evening.

She and I sat down on a cozy couch with Maxi in my lap and had a lovely conversation over a fresh glass of champagne. We talked about the dog show in Westminster where Maxi's victim was, for many years, involved as a judge. As she was getting up to leave, the woman gave Maxi a kind tug on the ear and said with a warm smile, "Maxi gets my vote."

Krakow

$\mathcal{B}$ACK IN ITALY, Ben appeared in a TV movie playing a small but central role in a special about the life and times of Pope John Paul II. Ben's work brought us to Rome, Italy and Krakow, Poland, the birthplace of the Pope, who was played as a young man by Cary

Elwes, and as a mature man, almost identically, by Jon Voight. I will never forget how sweet Jon was with Maxi. He always looked down at her and said, "Hi Shorty," but knowing Jon—a very tall man (both in spirit and heart)—anybody is "Shorty" next to him.

Arriving at the brand-new Sheraton Hotel in Krakow, Maxi was received with a big smile. Everyone from the receptionist to the waiters was very nice and made us feel welcome. I immediately asked for some newspapers for Maxi to do her business. The bellboy excused himself and handed me a good handful of the Polish paper of the day.

"That's all there is," he said. "*Polish News and Times*, would it be okay?" he asked.

"Of course," I said. "Our dog reads in every language."

We shared a nice laugh.

Spreading the paper in one of our bathrooms, my eye caught an adorable photo of a dachshund jumping over a big ball. From what I could make out, there would be a fair devoted to the dachshund in two weeks on a Sunday. At least a thousand wiener dogs were expected to show up and strut their stuff. It would take place in the market square, where much of the activity in Krakow occurred.

So, on our first day, Maxi and I took a stroll through the streets of Krakow until we came to big open space filled with people parading up and down, sitting in an outdoor restaurant, and listening to a band playing folklore music in the middle of the square. Many people were dressed in colorful folkloric outfits, with wreaths of flowers in their hair. What a charming city, I thought. The people couldn't be nicer. It was hard to believe these smiling, gracious people had been occupied and held prisoner first by Nazi Germany in 1939 then by Communist Russia until only recently. I wondered how many people had their courage. They greeted us often in German as though we were natives.

The day arrived for the dachshund fair, and I put Maxi's most colorful collar on with her leash, made of big plastic strawberries. We were ready to mingle. Maxi is a barker; when she sees other dogs, she speaks up and is sometimes a pain in the neck. But not this time. She was quiet and happy—her tail was wagging from side to side—it was as though she felt comfortable with her brothers and sisters.

The marketplace looked like a giant sausage factory; there were hundreds of dachshunds all around. One person after the other bent down to pet Maxi and admire her sweet little face and her especially beautiful sparkling eyes. I will always remember Krakow for the kindness of the people and how they appreciated our dog.

Paris Again

OUR NEXT LOCATION was Paris, where Ben worked on a film with Gérard Depardieu. His leading lady was Gena Rowlands. Ben and Gena have known each other for nearly forty years. Her husband, the late John Cassavetes, made some of Ben's finest movies and was

like family to us. Ben was excited to be working again with Gena; they are perfect together.

Maxi loves Paris and Paris loves dogs. Our hotel was the Plaza Athénée on the chic and exclusive Avenue Montaigne. We were greeted by a fat and jolly doorman. As Ben looked after the luggage, I told him I would meet him in the room, that I would take Maxi for a little walk. She had been traveling for hours and had not yet done her business. But what I really had my eye on was the Chanel shop across the street. Driving into the avenue, I looked to my left and there in Chanel's window was a stunning outfit I just had to try on. Paris was hot, steaming; you couldn't breathe. What a relief it was to enter the beautifully decorated, air-conditioned shop. Maxi's tail began wagging, as she jumped on a generously stuffed poof. She stretched out and watched me as I tried on outfit after outfit. Sometimes she cocked her head and looked at me as though to say, "Mommy, you are acting a little bananas." That's probably true; I was in a hurry to get back to Ben. I was a good girl; I only bought one out-fit. When it was time to leave, Maxi stopped dead, putting on her brakes in front of the big glass door. I pulled on her leash. But she sat and looked up at me as if to say, "Are you crazy, it's hot out there. I'm stay-ing inside. Basta."

The other customers in the store started to laugh, understanding the dog's position. One elegant lady said, *"Le chien et très intelligent."*

Ben and I always say that Paris is the best city in the world to walk in, even in the rain. Luckily, the weather was bearable the next day. So we walked for quite some time enjoying the sights and sounds of that beau-tiful city, including the Place Vendôme, the Tuileries, and the Palais Royal. All the while, Maxi saw a lot of her Parisian brothers and sisters.

We decided to have lunch on the Champs-Élysées at Fouquets, a restaurant we had frequented for many years. To avoid any problems, we placed Maxi in her carrying case before we entered. A cozy table was waiting for us. Happily, we ordered our drinks. While we enjoyed our chilled champagne, the waiter, without any question, put a third chair at our table, and said, "You can let the little animal out of the bag now. In Paris, we love dogs." I unzipped the bag and placed Maxi on the soft, red velvet chair. She sat like an angel. Then she looked from Ben to me. I knew what she wanted. Maxi was thirsty too. She wanted her champagne, which she really loves. At times, I let her lick some from my fingers. At that moment, the waiter appeared and put a bowl of fresh French water with an ice cube floating in the middle of it onto the floor. He smiled at Maxi and said, *"Voila, Mademoiselle Sante."*

Life was *très bien*—we had Maxi *and* Paris.

Maxi at the Ball

*B*EN AND I were invited to a charity event. Every year, our friends give the Food Allergy Initiative Ball in order to raise money to help find a cure for what can be a deadly condition. Just one peanut has been known to kill a person, adult or child. Foods we take for granted are a danger to many people.

We'd attended before, and I knew that the ladies would look their best. So I went first to my hairdresser, and Maxi watched from her carrying case as my hair was washed and blow dried. Very few beauty salons permit dogs, but Maxi has become an exception. When they were finished, I thanked everyone, put the leash on Maxi, and walked up Madison Avenue to my Korean girls. Maxi was also always welcome there.

The manicure took very little time and was well done, but what I was looking forward to was Kim and her pedicure, which I always found enormously relaxing.

"Ready for you, Mrs. Gazzara," she said.

While I sat in the high, plastic vibrating chair with my feet soaking in the warm, bubbly water, I heard a scratching sound. It was Maxi. She stood on her hind legs looking up at me with eyes that were hard to say no to.

"What is it, Maxi?" I asked.

She made a sweet pleading sound and I knew what it was. She wanted to sit in my lap. I asked permission and Kim nodded. Very soon, Maxi was dozing off and so was I. Kim has the touch. After finishing massaging my lower legs, she began pounding and punching them. My eyes opened. Maxi sprang up, barking loudly, putting her long nose up to Kim's face, and showing her long teeth. Poor Kim was shocked. The body cream and the pedicure tools went flying as she jumped up and ran to the other side of the room in fear. The other customers were first concerned and then amused by it all.

"Kim, she would never bite anyone," I said. "She thought you were hitting me and so was protecting me."

"I know, Mrs. Gazzara," said Kim, who was not convinced. I did not leave the nail parlor until there was peace between Kim and Maxi. I thanked her for being such a good sport, reached back in time, and said, "*Kamsamnida*," which means thank you in Korean. Kim smiled and asked where I'd learned it, and I told her I'd once spent four months in her country, which I remember fondly because that's where I met my husband.

"When?" asked Kim.

"Long before Maxi," I said.

OUR GERMAN DOG nanny, Maria, who had never let us down, was to arrive precisely at 6:30 P.M. She did not. I phoned her home and there was no answer. When it got to be 7:00, I turned to Ben and said, "*Lieber Gott im Himmel,* what are we going to do? We cannot take her into the Food Allergy Ball."

"We'll take her in the limousine and have the driver watch over her until we come out," said Ben.

"Excellent idea. Let's take her ball so she'll have something to play with."

"You're very smart."

Approaching the Hotel Pierre, Ben and I looked at each other and I said, "Why don't we put her in her Vuitton carrier and take her with us? Nobody will even notice."

"You're reading my mind."

He placed Maxi in her bag and zipped it up.

"Let's go, Maxi," I said. So we did.

The event was called an Italian Evening. There were chefs from famous restaurants giving advice on recipes that might benefit people with allergies. There was a tenor and soprano from the Met who performed. There were folk musicians dressed in velvet suits and berets who seemed to have walked out of a painting by an old master. There was champagne, every kind of spirits, and all sorts of Italian specialties to feast on. The flower centerpieces were gorgeous, and the table settings were generous, even extravagant.

As we sat at our table, we put Maxi and her carrying case on the floor between us. There was good food, the entertainment was lively, and the desert was fattening. Then came the speeches by the mothers and fathers of allergy victims. A very important man in the financial world came to the podium. With him was his much younger wife and a boy and a girl of about seven years of age. Uh-oh, I thought, this looks serious. And it was. The gentleman thanked everyone for being there, for helping in the battle against this condition that can often be fatal. He introduced his wife, the mother of his children, and the children themselves. He then told us about their struggles with allergies. I had no idea that so many people in the world had to be so careful about what they ate or drank.

The gentleman told us of the food his children could not eat, and added that even being near a dog or a cat would be extremely dangerous. I instinctively reached under the table to touch my Maxi, but the carrier was empty. Oh God, not again, I thought. She wasn't there. Where could she have gone? My heart began racing. If Maxi got too close to one of those children, they might get sick or die. The thought of it made me panic!

When I whispered to Ben that Maxi was missing, he sprang up and said, "I'll find her!" and started walking slowly around the ballroom, casually looking under chairs and asking waiters if they'd seen our little dog.

The room was filled with long tables, and ours was the longest. I carefully lifted the silk tablecloth, stuck my head under it, looked, and saw many legs and feet, but no Maxi. Trying not to make a scene, I got on my knees and ducked under the table. Crawling the entire length of it, I tried not to touch the guests who were still seated, having their after-dinner drinks. I went a long way on my hands and knees, and my body felt it. I was hot. My hair began to droop. What a mess. That's when I prayed, to Saint Vito, the protector of dogs, to bring Maxi back to me. Finally, I came up, gathered my composure, and sat down in my place. Others at the table asked me if I'd lost something. I looked around, thinking of what to do next, when, at the far end of the room, I saw Ben coming out of the kitchen. He very tenderly placed his hand on my cheek, and, straightening my messed-up hair, said, "Nobody's seen her."

I sank in my chair. I was becoming desperate. It was then I caught the eye of an attractive middle-aged man who waved at me as if asking me to come to him. I quickly moved in his direction, and when I got close, I saw her. My Maxi! She was sitting calmly in a thoroughly relaxed fashion in the smiling gentleman's arms.

"Mrs. Gazzara! Are you looking for your pooch?"

I was so happy that I said nothing. I bent down to take Maxi out of the stranger's arms and cradled her in mine. She licked my face, letting me know she was happy to see me.

"You're a bad girl," I said quietly. "Never do that again."

"She was simply exploring," said the kind gentleman.

"I'm so sorry."

"Don't worry, I won't tell anyone."

"I can't thank you enough."

"Yes, you can." He handed me his card and said, "Have your husband send me his autograph."

The Amazon

WE WERE INVITED to a film festival that took place in Manaus, the capital of the Amazon. I had been there before, but Ben hadn't. I will always have a warm spot in my heart for Brazil. I lived there for five years before I met Ben. I had two beautiful cocker spaniels at the time, and it almost killed me when I had to go back to Germany and leave them behind. At least I was able to leave them with a loving friend on her farm near São Paulo.

So, we decided to go to the festival. The question, as always, was would they allow dogs. They wouldn't. But the head of the festival pulled some political strings, and we were on our way. We flew from Rome to São Paulo—a twelve-hour flight—and then we flew four hours more to Manaus.

Maxi travels like a champion. The flight attendant pampered her with treat after treat. She was literally in heaven. In fact, Maxi was so comfortable in her carrying case that when we picked her up to

show her some action in the plane, she jumped right back into her little home.

When we arrived in São Paulo, we were led directly to the first-class lounge. There was everything your heart could desire. I had my *cafe zinho*, Ben had his beer, and Maxi her water. We found a cozy corner to sit in and placed Maxi between us on the floor. Then I heard someone calling out, "Ben, Ben."

It was Roman Polanski, who we had not seen since a lunch in Paris three years before. "Is that your dog?"

"Yeah," Ben said, "She's the love of my life."

"Next to your wife, I'm sure."

"Of course, everything is next to my wife."

"You'd better be careful in the Amazon," Roman said. "This is the monkey season. There are millions of them running around. They are small, but they are dangerous. They could easily attack your little hot dog."

"Now I am worried," I said. "Thank you for telling us."

"Just keep her close to you on her leash."

THE FESTIVAL WASN'T bad. The films were shown in the famous opera house that was built by a very wealthy plantation owner who had a love for opera. They say the Great Caruso sang there. The interior was gold leaf with murals of famous composers looking down from the gilded ceiling. The films in competition were not particularly special, but there were some that were interesting. Ben was there to be a judge along with director Norman Jewison, actress Claudia Cardinale, and others. Roman's new film, *Oliver Twist*, was shown out of competition and got a lot of attention.

Maxi attended most of the films but wasn't so happy and neither were we. The air conditioning had us shivering. We kept each other warm. I pressed her body against mine like a hot water bottle.

I sure didn't need a hot water bottle on our tour of the Amazon though. One day, an old steamboat was moored in the canal near our hotel. It was only 8:00 A.M., but the heat felt like an oven. I wanted to jump in a cold shower and stay there all day. Instead, we got on a boat and sailed into a sweltering, humid day down the river into the rainforests.

When the boat stopped, Ben was the first one off and I handed Maxi to him as I got off so she wouldn't escape into the jungle. We walked to the hotel, which was actually structured houses built into the trees. We were assigned to one of the prime tree houses, and we loved it. We were looking forward to living the simple life. Maxi was excited. She must have smelled the presence of other animals.

That night, there was a party in our honor given by the owner of the hotel who was known as the king of the Amazon. The evening was spectacular. A Brazilian dance group from Rio performed beautifully. They were dressed in sparkling outfits with boas and feathers. Some were fully dressed, and some weren't dressed at all. Many of the *mulatas* in the show asked Maxi to dance. She never refused. Maxi loves the Brazilian beat.

When we headed back to the tree house at around 2:00 A.M., it started to rain—a light rain. We prepared Maxi's bed in a big chair, which we pulled near to our raw lumber bed. It didn't take long. We watched as Maxi made herself comfortable and went to sleep. The room was air conditioned, and it seemed like a freezer to me, so we bundled Maxi up with a blanket, covered ourselves with everything available, and went to sleep. I don't know how long I had been sleeping when Maxi barked. I heard strange noises coming from the roof louder and louder. Raccoons again, I wondered, or tropical rain? By that time, Ben had woken up. "What's going on?"

"It's raining cats and dogs," I said.

"Well let's take a look."

We opened the door, and there was a not a cloud in the sky—and not a drop of rain. As soon as Maxi and I stepped out to look up to the roof, there was a sudden stampede—a swarm—there were maybe a hundred little wild monkeys running on the roof, obviously figuring out a way to escape before they were devoured by our big, bad dog.

That morning at breakfast, we told the story to Roman. He leaned in close to Maxi and said, "No monkey business here, right Maxi? No monkey business."

Maxi licked his face.

Athens

$\mathcal{I}$NVITATIONS TO FILM festivals just kept coming. Ben and I were in Italy when we received an invitation to take part in the Athens Film Festival. Before our lives were blessed with Maxi, we had been there once, but only briefly, and were delighted to hear that this time, we would be able to spend at least four days there. They were going to be showing two of Ben's movies, and I knew he would be occupied with press conferences and the like, giving Maxi and me time to ourselves.

We stayed in a lovely hotel in the "Beverly Hills" section of the city. Our spacious suite had a splendid view of the Acropolis, which made us happy but Maxi even happier with all the room she had for playing with her ball—not only the rooms, but also the balcony that circled the entire suite.

The day after we arrived, Ben had a number of meetings to attend, so I thought I'd wander around the city's famous shopping area. Ben

dropped me and Maxi at its center, and he said he'd phone me before lunchtime.

Holding Maxi by her colorful red leash, I began browsing and was surprised by the quality of the merchandise. I was also surprised by the sudden attention. Person after person, men and women, stopped to point at Maxi and admire her. One elderly lady squatted and began petting Maxi, who obviously did not like the woman. She started to growl. I became concerned and picked Maxi up before she showed her teeth and frightened the poor woman to death.

I found an outdoor café and sat for some time, but no phone call from Ben. I knew he must be trying and that it had to be that my Italian phone was not receiving calls. I ordered a Greek salad and a glass of wine and asked the young waiter to bring Maxi some water. He said he could not serve a dog. So I asked him to bring me a bottle of mineral water. I saw there was an ashtray on the table and that it was clean, perfect for my darling dog to drink from. There are ashtrays on all the tables in Greece. Wherever you look, people have cigarettes in their mouths, smoking like chimneys.

It was now 4:00 P.M. and still no call. I moved to a taxi stand with Maxi in my arms. There was a very long line, but it moved quickly, because three, four, and even five people would share the same cab. When it came to my turn, one taxi after another passed me by, many drivers shaking their heads and mumbling something in Greek, which of course I didn't understand. I felt like an idiot. Finally, the driver of one passing cab said in English, "No dok, no dok!" I moved quickly, taking my leather jacket and wrapping it around Maxi as they do salami. I was determined to hide her, and I was getting nervous. Ben's movie would be shown in two hours, and I had to get back to the

hotel. I had a sheet of my hotel stationery to show the driver; otherwise, I would never have been able to tell him where I was heading.

Finally, a cab driver stopped for me. He was a very handsome man, who resembled a Greek I'd known well, our dear friend John Cassavetes. He asked where I was from.

"Germany," I said.

"I thought so, which city madam?"

"Hannover."

"Hannovero," he said. "That's ancient Greek."

When we arrived at the hotel, the cab driver turned around, smiled, and looked down at my jacket. "What's the name of your little hot dog?" he asked.

"Oh, you saw her. Sorry. This is Maxi," I said proudly.

He turned around further in his seat, reached out, and gently pushed back my leather jacket. Maxi's sweet head peeked out ever so slowly. He caressed her, placed two of his fingers on his lips, and then ran them along Maxi's long nose. His eyes were full of tenderness when he looked at her and said, "*Sagapo*, Maxi."

He told her he loved her.

BEN'S MOVIE WAS very well received, and it brought back a lot of memories. We celebrated the evening with our old and new Greek friends. It was a big, generous Greek dinner, followed by music with lots of dancing and singing. During the evening, one of our friends asked Maxi to dance. He lifted her out of her carrying case and took her to the stage. Very soon, one man after the other joined our friend Phedon and our baby on the dance floor. Maxi was the only girl and seemed to be enjoying all the attention she was getting.

I think I even saw her smile.

Sag Harbor

*C*HRISTINE AND MICHAEL Namer, our ex-Sag Harbor neighbors, invited me and Maxi to spend the weekend in their home there, which is directly across the street from where we used to live. Ben was in Guatemala shooting a movie. Maxi and I wouldn't be joining him for another week, so I accepted the invitation.

It was an unbearably hot Friday afternoon. I was a bit early coming downstairs, so I dropped my bag and Maxi's carrying case in our air-conditioned lobby. It was hell outside, an inferno. There seemed to be no air to breathe. As I was heading back into my building, a car pulled up and the door of the driver's side flew open. Thinking it was Michael, I let Maxi go and she headed full speed for the car and jumped in. "Michael," I shouted, "I hope your air conditioning is working." But it wasn't Michael. It was a handsome-looking gentleman whose face was familiar. He was the Vice Consul General of Italy who was at my table at a recent dinner party.

"I'm afraid I won't have the pleasure of being your chauffeur, Mrs. Gazzara."

"Oh, I'm so sorry Mr. Stefano," I said. "The heat is getting to me."

At that point, Maxi jumped back out of the car. The gentlemen bent to pet her. He said that a good friend of his who lives nearby has dogs very much like Maxi.

"Actually," he said, "they belong to his mother, Mrs. Brooke Astor. My friend is her son."

I knew those dogs. On a few occasions, I'd even had a conversation with their dog walker. Only recently, he'd told me about Mrs. Astor's upcoming 104th birthday. He described how much she loved her dogs and how they were aging along with her. I thought how happy I would be to have Maxi to keep me company for many years to come. Although Maxi doesn't like many dogs, she actually nuzzled up to one of Mrs. Astor's dogs and then the other, and they carried on a silent conversation.

I sent Mrs. Astor a "warm hug" for each of her dogs. I chose a beautiful wine red sweater for the boy and a bright red one for the girl. I'd seen the impressive lady only recently getting out of a limousine. The chauffeur opened the back door and out came two handsome dachshunds on their leashes. The doorman picked up their leashes and walked them into the building. He returned in time to assist an elegantly dressed lady wearing hat and gloves step gingerly out of the car and walk regally into her building. I felt that time had stopped, that I was watching a silent movie star.

Some days later, I received a note from Mrs. Astor's son thanking me on behalf of his mother. "She was so pleased by your two magnificent Italian dog sweaters," he wrote. "God bless you and Maxi." That family has style, I thought.

WHEN MICHAEL FINALLY arrived in his Range Rover, we left the broiling city behind us. I sat in the backseat with Maxi at my side. The air conditioning was blowing ice-cold air. I covered Maxi with my jean jacket, and she fell asleep right away. When we arrived on the country road leading to Sag Harbor, I saw that the spacious potato fields were covered with houses. The little fruit and vegetable stands had become enclosed stores. And the traffic on Scuttle Hole Road was the same as you'd find in a big city. How disappointing.

As we got closer to our old street, my denim jacket started moving. Maxi's head appeared and she stood up with her two paws, resting the other two on my lap. Her head was glued to the glass. She knew we were on our way home. I opened the car window and she smelled the Sag Harbor air, her long brown nose stretched out the window, seeming to get longer with every sniff. Her little ears were flying in the evening wind, her busy tail was drumming strongly and excitedly on my chest and stomach. She gave a happy, girlish yelp.

Here's where it had all started, where little baby Maxi came with my daughter Danja and us to our cozy home. It was winter, and to see this little animal jump up and down in the white powdered snow much like a kangaroo was amusing and touching at the same time. Ben had made it clear that it was all right to spend a bit of time with this dog, but he was definitely against having it come to live with us. We were together for four days. I remember it was a particularly beautiful winter. The days were full of sunshine. Ben would take his morning coffee and paper, sit on the front porch, and watch Maxi as she cavorted in the snow. One morning, he got in the car and drove to town without telling me why he was leaving. He was soon back with a paper bag from which he retrieved a rubber ball that made a squeaking sound. When Maxi heard the first squeak, she became more excited than I'd ever seen her. Ben threw the ball. She'd retrieve it. He'd throw it again. And she'd retrieve it again. It became their game.

Ben fell in love with Maxi, and she quickly became a member of our family. It felt like only yesterday that we had to introduce her carefully to the open swimming pool. I got an inflatable chair and placed Maxi into the spacious rubber chair. Her big brown eyes were full of fear. She clung to my wet bathing suit. Bringing her close to my breast, I walked slowly down the steps to the shallow part of the swimming pool. She was trembling—it was clear to me then that Maxi would never be a water dog.

As we approached Sag Harbor, Michael's car slowed down. We passed the lake filled with ducks and the lovely, lush park that took us into our old street, which ends in a cul-de-sac. By now, it was early evening. I quickly took Maxi in my arms so she wouldn't glance over to our old house and run to see it. But she was not fooled. Her beautiful dark eyes never stopped looking at it.

Early the next morning, before anyone was up, Maxi was already scratching at the door ready to go out and explore. I got dressed quickly and opened the main door. Maxi literally flew over the lawn, up the stairway, and looked through the low window of our former house. She barked as if to say, "This is my house, open the door." She waited, thought a moment, turned away from the door, and disappeared under the house. Soon she reappeared, proudly holding a soft green rubber ball in her mouth. It still squeaked. It had been there for at least two years, but our little hunting dog went right to it. With the ball in her mouth, she moved toward the pool area and then she stopped suddenly. The pool was gone. Instead there stood a brand-new, not-so-pretty white mansion waiting for a foolish buyer.

Maxi was obviously confused. She turned her back and moved into the vast backyard. While smelling the plants and flowers, she would occasionally squat and mark the territory that once belonged to her. She then led me around the house to our rolling front yard where she and Ben had enjoyed playing with her ball. Those days are gone, I thought to myself. Maxi still had important things on her mind. She walked toward our long graveled driveway. When she arrived at what years ago had been one of her favorite spots, Maxi performed her ritual dance filled with turns and spins. Finally the moment came, and she looked up to me as she squatted in what had been her own personal outdoor powder room. It was then that she left her most important mark.

When we returned to the city, as soon as I opened the door to our Madison Avenue apartment, Maxi jumped out of her case carrying in her mouth the green ball she had retrieved after so many years. She ran with her long lost property under our bed, playing with it until dinner time. I took that moment to steal the ball and hide it in my luggage for Guatemala. I knew Ben would get a kick out of it.

It was a very early flight, so we had to be ready to leave the house at 6:00 A.M. I looked for Maxi in her bed, in the den, and in the bathroom; I called her name, but no answer. I walked into the foyer and there she was sitting on the very piece of luggage where I had hidden her ball. Her little head moved to one side as though she were asking, "Why are you tormenting me?"

Antigua

*T*HE FLIGHT FROM New York to Guatemala City took some four and a half hours, and Maxi rested in her carrying case for most of it. The flight attendants were particularly sweet with her. They brought her water, and when they heard she loves raw carrots, they produced one. We were flying business class, but it was first-class treatment.

When we got to Passport Control, I looked toward the waiting area where Ben had informed me that a dark and handsome young man carrying a sign with my name on it would be picking us up. My passport had no sooner been stamped than Maxi leapt out of her case and raced toward the people waiting for their loved ones. It was at least a hundred yards away, but she made it in three seconds, flying into the arms of someone she knew very well. It was Ben. He'd come, roses in hand, to surprise us. As I approached, Maxi was still licking his face, and I gave him a big kiss, too.

The drive from Guatemala City to our hotel was uneventful and not

particularly pleasing to the eye. But after an hour's drive, we came upon a lush, green valley that brought us to Antigua, a city of multicolored buildings no more than one story high. It sits at 4,000 feet under three volcanoes, and its weather is temperate and glorious all year long. Many people come for a visit and remain forever.

When we got to the hotel, the driver helped me because I was carrying Maxi in my arms. Ben was busy collecting my luggage.

"Jesus Christ, Elke, what did you put in this luggage? I can't lift it."

"It has all Maxi's food in it," I said smiling.

As I walked through the front door leading to the reception desk, a dark-skinned man with Mayan features stopped me and said, *"No perros, senora, aqui no perros,"* pointing to a sign of a dog with a thick black line drawn across it. I called for Ben.

"Ben, please help. We have a big problem here."

Ben, using a mélange of Spanish, Italian, and English, was able to explain that Maxi had been cleared to stay at the Hotel Porta Antigua until the end of the filming of the movie he was working on. And so it was another first. Maxi is the only dog ever allowed at a first-class hotel in Antigua and probably the last.

One morning, Ben had to leave for work earlier than usual. I had my breakfast near the pool while Maxi played with her ball on the big green lawn. A group of hotel guests approached me asking about Maxi's breed and how old she was.

"Que lindo, que bonito!"

So I said, *"Que linda, que bonita, she is a girl."*

At exactly that moment, one of two big, beautifully feathered parrots that were perched nearby jumped from his perch and, though his wings were clipped, was able to fly at least five feet off the ground, landing smack in the middle of Maxi's back, covering her entirely with his red, gold, and blue feathers. Maxi looked over her shoulder and acted puzzled by the visit. She seemed to be asking, "What the heck are you doing here?" The bird let out a loud croak. Maxi let out an even louder bark. The bird left Maxi's back and flew two or three feet off the ground back toward his perch. Maxi went in the opposite direction, even leaving her beloved ball behind. She had a lot to think about. I believe that she and the bird were both in shock. My heart was racing. It could have been a tragedy, I thought.

Early the next morning, Maxi and I were on the lawn again. I did not see the bird keeper as he uncovered the parrot's cages and placed a long pole for them to step on so that he could carry them to their tree.

When I finally saw what was happening, I retrieved Maxi's ball and was bending over to attach her leash to her collar, when I felt a strong wind blowing across my face. It was the male parrot that had visited with Maxi the morning before. This time, he landed right in front of Maxi and simply stared at her. Maxi stared back. I thought, This could be Ingrid Bergman looking at Humphrey Bogart in the last scene of *Casablanca*. I think that parrot had a crush on Maxi, and she must have thought he was pretty cute, too.

That day, Ben and I took our first stroll into town, walking the cobblestone streets of Antigua's Fifth Avenue. As we walked underneath the ancient arcade, a good-looking elderly gentleman, wearing a cowboy hat and a bright scarf around his neck, stopped his white station wagon and, pointing to Maxi, said, "Those are the greatest dogs in the world."

"Do you have one?" I asked.

"I had two." He looked down at Maxi and suddenly his eyes filled with tears. He shook his head and drove away, obviously remembering.

Ben said, "That's a small example of what would happen to us if we ever lost Maxi."

Antigua is a city of dogs. They come in all sizes. Some walk on a leash with their owners, many of them wander around without even a collar. Like the people in Antigua, they are all sweet and friendly. Every home we were invited to had at least three or four dogs, and they were often very big and always gentle. Those animals are treated very well. They were always kind and considerate with Maxi.

On a beautiful Sunday afternoon, we were invited for lunch by Álvaro Arzú, the ex-president of Guatemala, his wife Patricia, and his sister Mercedes. As he approached us, surrounded by twelve enormous German shepherds, he saluted. Maxi started growling and moving toward them, and then she began barking so loud that the big dogs backed up. They were surprised that a dog so small could make such a racket. She almost pulled me away. My heart was racing. The big boys looked down at her, as though to say, "Are you silly? Don't you know how small you are?" Our host took control of the situation and told his workers to put the dogs away, behind a fenced-in grassy area.

By then, however, Maxi had decided that she liked them. She pulled on her leash, indicating that I should let her go play with her new German friends. Not on your life, I thought. "You stay right here *Mein Fraulein*." We had a divine lunch, a lot of laughs, and even a juicy carrot for Maxi. When it was over, she didn't want to leave. Maxi is an only child, and I think she wanted the company of her new friends. Even she sometimes feels lonely.

Going Home

RIVING OVER THE Triborough Bridge toward Manhattan, Maxi jumped up and rested her paws on the windowsill, probably to get a better look at the magnificent New York City skyline. Every time we approach New York, Maxi experiences the same excitement. She knows, as I do, that we are going home.

Deep down in her heart, Maxi is a New York dog. She seems to come alive in the streets of the city, passing the chic and expensive boutiques that sell the latest fashion from all over the world and the crowded art galleries and indoor and outdoor restaurants. She gladly escorts us to our bank, our bread store, our pastry baker, our shoe-maker, our local bookshop, our fruit and vegetable man, and our old-fashioned pharmacy. But most importantly, she escorts us to our doctors. They all seem to be situated near our home. Maxi often leads us straight to their door, and she is always welcome. So long as she is in her carrying case, most doctors and nurses are very fond of her. But

while lying and spying out of her carrying case, some doctors don't even know she is in the room.

The doctors who do know, however, always say, as I am leaving the office, "Good-bye Elke." And then they quietly bend down and say with a knowing smile, "Good-bye Maxi."

When we are outside, Maxi's strut seems to take on an extra sense of pride, even nobility. She knows she's back on Madison Avenue.

SOMETIMES I'M REMINDED so suddenly how much Maxi means to Ben and me and what our lives would look like without her. One day recently, pulling ahead of me on her leash, Maxi almost got hit by a car—a crazy taxi driver was trying to beat the traffic light. I was scared to death. I moved quickly, dropping my phone, my handbag, and my shopping bags—everything I had in my hands—and I scooped Maxi up into my shaking arms. Both of our hearts were beating furiously. Ben gathered my things from the ground, came closer to me, and said, "Shhhh, take a deep breath, Maxi knows you saved her life." As I caressed her, she looked at me with such affection, as if to say, "Thank you Mom."

We continued our walk for a few moments, and then we took a little moment to sit on a bench outside a local restaurant. The cool afternoon sun was shining right on Maxi's sweet face. I looked into her eyes and found it hard to believe that our little girl had come into our lives eight years ago. She was still as playful and lively as the tiny puppy named Max we met over lunch nearly a decade ago. Placing Maxi back on the sidewalk, we moved slowly up Madison Avenue to our building.

"Ben, I never get tired of watching Maxi's proud walk—her wiggling tail, her windblown floppy ears, and her strong, crooked gait. What would we have done if we had lost her?"

"I don't even want to think about it."

I looked down at this adorable animal who had captured our hearts from the start; from the very first day she came to live with us, we became different people. She brought out all of our tenderness and affection. Without even noticing it, Ben and I became more loving and kinder to each other, and our arguments became very brief because Maxi doesn't approve of angry and loud voices. In nearly every way, Maxi became our child.

And now her tiny paws and chin are turning gray—time leaves marks on everyone—but Maxi doesn't pay attention to time, God bless her. We watch her with pleasure as she plays, eats, sleeps, and even when she makes her business. Maxi is the love of our lives. We grow old together.